AS/A-LEVEL
Pure Mathematics
Robert Smedley

Exam Revision Notes

Dedicated to my parents

Philip Allan Updates
Market Place
Deddington
Oxfordshire
OX15 0SE

tel: 01869 338652
fax: 01869 337590
e-mail: sales@philipallan.co.uk
www.philipallan.co.uk

ISBN 0 86003 438 0

Cover illustration by John Spencer
Printed by Raithby, Lawrence & Co Ltd, Leicester

AS/A-Level Pure Mathematics

Contents

Introduction

These revision notes cover the AS/A2 pure mathematics core material in a concise format. For each topic, they provide key definitions, results and techniques as well as numerous worked examples. These worked examples illustrate the applications and follow typical exam question styles.

The first topic, Algebra, covers all the 'basic' algebraic tools that you will need and assumes appropriate GCSE knowledge.

It is assumed that the reader is following an AS/A2 course and is therefore covering detailed explanations and proofs.

How you might use this book

The specification that you are following will be unique to your particular examination board. A good starting point is to go through this book marking those topics that are not included in your particular specification. This will be a small amount of material and might only involve the exclusion of some of the sub-sections. However, starting with this exercise will enable you to become familiar with the list of topics that you need to cover for revision as well as ensuring that you do not revise material that is not relevant to your examination!

This book aids revision by splitting each topic into sections. Look through the key point(s) and then try the associated worked example(s). A good technique is to cover up the solution, try the example for yourself and then compare your solution with the one provided. This technique will help you to identify whether or not reinforcement or further work is needed.

Some of the topics are short (e.g. binomial expansions) and could be tackled in one revision session. In the case of some of the longer topics, such as trigonometry, it is advisable to work in smaller sections.

The book will be very useful for reference purposes as it enables you to dip into topics as and when required.

Revising for the mathematics examination

Although we all learn and revise in different ways, there are some useful tips to be learnt about revising mathematics effectively. Mathematics is not a spectator sport — it is crucial to practise at the revision stage rather than simply reading notes. This book has been written to assist you in this style of revision.

The following example shows why this approach is important. After reading through your notes, you might decide that you know the formula for finding the distance between two points with co-ordinates (x_1, y_1) and (x_2, y_2).

$$d = \sqrt{(x_2 - x_1)^2 + (y_2 - y_1)^2}$$

But do you know how to *use* the formula and *apply* it, which is what an examination question will require you to do?

An examination question requiring the use of this formula might:

- involve negative coordinates, which need extra care with the negative signs. For example, using the coordinates $(-3, 7)$ and $(4, -1)$ would give

$$d = \sqrt{(4 - (-3))^2 + (-1 - 7)^2}$$

Mistakes manipulating negative signs are very common and result in the unnecessary loss of marks.

- give the coordinates of the three vertices of a triangle and require you to show that the triangle is isosceles. In this case, you need to identify that this formula is to be used to calculate the lengths of the sides of the triangle and then you have to use the formula.

At the revision stage, you may revise discrete topics and feel confident that you understand the topic in detail. However, examination questions do not necessarily focus on discrete topics. For example, in this book there is a section on 'use of partial fractions to obtain series expansions'. Similarly, partial fractions are used to split algebraic fractions and express them in a form that enables them to be integrated easily.

In the case of quadratic inequalities, the technique shown in this book is to sketch the graph of the quadratic function in the region of its intersection with the x-axis. To do this you need to be able to identify key features of a quadratic graph from a given equation.

All these intricacies can only be identified and tackled effectively through practice and 'doing' questions. For this reason, it is crucial to go through numerous past examination papers once you are confident that you understand all the relevant material.

When tackling past examination papers, this book will be a valuable reference. For example, if you attempt an examination question on vectors which presents the vector equation of a plane in a particular form, but you cannot remember the key aspects of the form, turn to Topic 12. The relevant section presents all three forms concisely, together with key aspects of each.

The examination
- Read the question carefully — do not assume anything about it. For example, compare the following questions:

  - Differentiate $f(x) = x^2$ from first principles and hence find the gradient of the curve $f(x) = x^2$ at the point $(-2, 4)$.

  - Calculate the gradient of the curve defined by $f(x) = x^2$ at the point $(-2, 4)$.

The first requires something different and more than the second. In the case of the first, the differentiation is to be performed via the definition

$$f'(x) = \lim_{h \to 0} \left\{ \frac{f(x + h) - f(x)}{h} \right\}$$

whereas in the second question, the standard result for first derivative can be used.

Some questions may look similar to those that you have tried during your revision but it does not mean that they are identical. This is a common error and can easily be avoided. For instance, you should understand the difference between a question that asks

- Complete the table of values and plot the points...

and a question that asks

- Sketch the graph of $y =$...

During your revision you might attempt the following question:

- The number of bacteria N present at any time t hours after the beginning of an experiment is increasing at a rate proportional to its present size. Show that

    $N = Ae^{kt}$

    where A and k are constants. Given that...

In the examination, the following question might appear:

- The number of bacteria present at time t hours after the beginning of an experiment is denoted by N. The relationship between N and t is denoted by

    $N = 100e^{\frac{3t}{2}}$

    After how many hours...

A common error is *not* to read the question carefully and to proceed to derive the relationship $N = Ae^{kt}$ from the differential equation $\frac{dN}{dt} = kN$, which is the derivation you have learnt! However, this would achieve zero marks as the question gives the relationship as $N = 100e^{\frac{3t}{2}}$ and then requires candidates to use this.

- Always start with a question you feel confident about. Completing a question at the start of an exam can really boost your confidence. For example, a question such as

    - Differentiate $y = x\ln x$ with respect to x

    might only be worth 3 marks, but it is straightforward differentiation using the product rule and one that should not present any problems.

- Do not waste time struggling with a question that you are unsure about when there are others on the paper that you know how to answer.

- Always keep an eye on the clock. During the revision stage of answering past examination questions you must time yourself and work out approximately how much time to allocate to questions/sections.

- The way in which you lay out your solutions is an important part of mathematics and you must be precise. A common error is to write working in a 'sloppy' fashion, which results in incorrect mathematics. For example, consider the question

    - Given that $f(x) = 3x^2 - x + 1$, evaluate $f(-2)$.

A 'sloppy' approach to this might be:

$f(-2) = 3(-2)^2 = 12 - (-2) = 14 + 1 = 15$

resulting in a correct answer of 15 but an incorrect mathematical statement. The correct approach is to write

$f(-2) = 3(-2)^2 - (-2) + 1$
$= 12 + 2 + 1$
$\therefore \quad f(-2) = 15$

- Longer questions comprise different parts and in some cases the marks at the end are harder to obtain than the marks at the beginning. Therefore, if you have not completed the paper do not waste time trying to obtain 3 'difficult' marks at the end of a question when the first 3 marks of the next question are straightforward.

- You must remember that no matter how much revision you do and how many past examination papers you complete, a question may appear on your paper that does not look like anything you have seen before. In these cases you are required to apply your knowledge and skills. For example, you may have revised 'standard' quadratic equations thoroughly, gone through the section in this book in detail and then the following question appears on your examination paper:

  - Solve the equation $e^{2x} - 4e^x + 3 = 0$

  The skill here is to recognise that this is a quadratic equation in e^x, i.e.

  $$(e^x)^2 - 4(e^x) + 3 = 0$$

  Letting $y = e^x$ gives

  $$y^2 - 4y + 3 = 0$$

  which can now be solved for y by factorising.

- There are numerous careless errors and misconceptions that candidates make in examinations. A final revision tip that I guarantee you will find useful is to identify those errors that *you* tend to make over and over again. Constructing such a list for yourself will enable you to focus on correcting such errors. Such a list might contain some of the following common errors:

  - $(x - y)^2 = x^2 + y^2$

  - If $x(x+3) = 4$ then $x = 4$ or $x + 3 = 4$

  - $\sqrt{1 - \sin^2\theta} = 1 - \sin\theta$

  - $\int \sin^2 x \, dx = \dfrac{\sin^3 x}{3} + c$

  - $\sin(\theta + 30°) = \sin\theta + \sin 30°$

  - $\int \dfrac{1}{x} \, dx = \int x^{-1} \, dx = \dfrac{x^0}{0} + c = 1$

  - $\int_{30°}^{60°} \cos x \, dx$. (The limits on definite integrals involving trigonometric functions must be in radians.)

I hope you find this book useful and that it helps you achieve success in your mathematics AS/A-level. The best of luck!

Robert Smedley

TOPIC 1 Algebra

1 Indices

For integers m and n:

- $x^m \times x^n = x^{m+n}$

- $x^m \div x^n = x^{m-n}$

- $(x^m)^n = x^{mn}$

Example

Simplify $\dfrac{2x^5 \times x}{x^2}$.

Solution

Using the first result to simplify the numerator, gives $\dfrac{2x^6}{x^2}$

Using the second result to perform the division, gives $2x^4$

Note: a common simplification error is illustrated by the example $3^4 \times 5^2 = 15^6$. This is clearly not true. However, $3^4 \times 3^2 = 3^6$ is true.

1.1 NEGATIVE AND FRACTIONAL INDICES

- $x^{-m} = \dfrac{1}{x^m}$
- $x^{\frac{1}{n}} = \sqrt[n]{x}$
- $x^{\frac{m}{n}} = \sqrt[n]{x^m}$

Example

Simplify   (i) 5^{-2} (ii) $27^{-\frac{1}{3}}$ (iii) $\left(\dfrac{1}{9}\right)^{\frac{1}{2}}$

Solution

(i) $5^{-2} = \dfrac{1}{5^2} = \dfrac{1}{25}$

(ii) $27^{-\frac{1}{3}} = \dfrac{1}{27^{\frac{1}{3}}} = \dfrac{1}{\sqrt[3]{27}} = \dfrac{1}{3}$

(iii) $\left(\dfrac{1}{9}\right)^{\frac{1}{2}} = \sqrt{\dfrac{1}{9}} = \dfrac{1}{3}$

Example

Simplify $\dfrac{2q^3 \times (5q^{-5})^2}{q}$.

Solution

Simplifying the numerator gives $\dfrac{2q^3 \times 25q^{-10}}{q} = \dfrac{50q^{-7}}{q}$

Now, performing the division gives $50q^{-8}$

This could be also written as $50\dfrac{1}{q^8}$ or $\dfrac{50}{q^8}$

2 | *Surds*

Roots such as $\sqrt{2}$, $\sqrt{3}$, $\sqrt{5}$, ... are called surds. They are irrational numbers, i.e. they cannot be expressed as a fraction of two integers. For example, $\sqrt{25}$ is not a surd since $\sqrt{25} = 5 = \frac{5}{1}$, i.e. a fraction of two integers.

2.1 PROPERTIES OF SURDS

- $\sqrt{a} \times \sqrt{b} = \sqrt{ab}$

- $\dfrac{\sqrt{a}}{\sqrt{b}} = \sqrt{\dfrac{a}{b}}$

Example

Simplify $\sqrt{32}$.

Solution

Looking for the largest square factor of 32, namely 16, gives

$$\sqrt{32} = \sqrt{16 \times 2} = \sqrt{16} \times \sqrt{2} = 4\sqrt{2}$$

Example

Simplify $\sqrt{18} + \sqrt{2} - \sqrt{8}$.

Solution

In each case look for the largest square factor and simplify. This gives

$$\sqrt{9 \times 2} + \sqrt{2} - \sqrt{4 \times 2} = 3\sqrt{2} + \sqrt{2} - 2\sqrt{2} = 2\sqrt{2}$$

2.2 RATIONALISING SURDS

If surds appear in the denominator of a fraction, it is common practice to rewrite the fraction by rationalising the denominator.

To rationalise the fraction $\dfrac{1}{a \pm \sqrt{b}}$, multiply numerator and denominator by $a \mp \sqrt{b}$.

The following examples illustrate some different types of rationalisation question.

Example

Rationalise $\dfrac{1}{\sqrt{5}}$.

Solution

In this case, multiply numerator and denominator by $\sqrt{5}$, which is equivalent to multiplying by 1. This gives

$$\frac{1}{\sqrt{5}} \times \frac{\sqrt{5}}{\sqrt{5}} = \frac{\sqrt{5}}{5} = \frac{1}{5}\sqrt{5}$$

Note: examination questions tend not to use the word rationalise. They ask for answers to be expressed in the form $a + b\sqrt{c}$ and candidates are required to make the connection with the rationalisation process. The following example illustrates this.

Example

Express $\dfrac{1}{1 + \sqrt{5}}$ in the form $a + b\sqrt{5}$.

Solution

In this case, the first step is to rationalise, i.e. multiply numerator and denominator by $1 - \sqrt{5}$, giving

$$\frac{1}{1 + \sqrt{5}} \times \frac{1 - \sqrt{5}}{1 - \sqrt{5}} = \frac{1 - \sqrt{5}}{1 - \sqrt{5} + \sqrt{5} - 5}$$

$$= \frac{1 - \sqrt{5}}{-4}$$

$$= -\frac{1}{4} + \frac{1}{4}\sqrt{5}$$

Here, $a = -\dfrac{1}{4}$ and $b = \dfrac{1}{4}$

Examples may involve surds in both the numerator and denominator.

Example

Express $\dfrac{1 + \sqrt{3}}{2 - \sqrt{3}}$ in the form $a + b\sqrt{3}$.

Solution

The first step is to rationalise, giving

$$\frac{1 + \sqrt{3}}{2 - \sqrt{3}} \times \frac{2 + \sqrt{3}}{2 + \sqrt{3}} = \frac{2 + \sqrt{3} + 2\sqrt{3} + 3}{4 + 2\sqrt{3} - 2\sqrt{3} - 3}$$

$$= \frac{5 + 3\sqrt{3}}{1}$$

$$= 5 + 3\sqrt{3}$$

The required form is $5 + 3\sqrt{3}$

3   Logarithms

If $y = a^x$ then x is said to be the logarithm (log for short) of y to the base a. We write $x = \log_a y$. The following numerical examples illustrate this more clearly:

- $8 = 2^3$ can be written as $3 = \log_2 8$
- $1000 = 10^3$ can be written as $3 = \log_{10} 1000$

Note: $\log_2 2 = 1$, $\log_{10} 10 = 1$.

Generally, $\log_a a = 1$.

Most calculators only have the function keys $\log_{10}$ and $\log_e$, where $e = 2.718$ to three decimal places.

3.1 NOTATION

We write $\log_e x = \ln x$.

3.2 PROPERTIES OF LOGARITHMS

* $\log xy = \log x + \log y$
* $\log \left(\dfrac{x}{y} \right) = \log x - \log y$
* $\log x^n = n \log x$

These are very useful properties which can be used to simplify expressions involving logarithms.

Example

Simplify:

(i) $\log 9 - \log 3$

(ii) $3 \log 2 + \log 5$

Solution

(i) Using the second property gives

$$\log 9 - \log 3 = \log \left(\frac{9}{3} \right)$$
$$= \log 3$$

An alternative approach is

$$\log 9 - \log 3 = \log 3^2 - \log 3$$
$$= 2 \log 3 - \log 3$$
$$= \log 3$$

Clearly the first method is simpler but both are correct.

(ii) Using the third property, with the expression $3 \log 2$, gives $\log 2^3 = \log 8$. Then, using the first property gives

$$3 \log 2 + \log 5 = \log 8 + \log 5$$
$$= \log (8 \times 5)$$
$$= \log 40$$

3.3 SOLVING EQUATIONS INVOLVING LOGARITHMS

Logs are a useful tool when it comes to solving equations in which the unknown is the index.

Example

Solve the equation $5^x = 30$.

Solution

The first step is to take logs of both sides (base 10 or e, since these are the two bases available on the calculator). This gives

$$\log 5^x = \log 30$$

Now using the third property gives

$$x \log 5 = \log 30$$
$$\therefore \quad x = \frac{\log 30}{\log 5} = 2.113 \ (3\,\text{dp})$$

A common error is to write $\dfrac{\log 30}{\log 5} = \log\left(\dfrac{30}{5}\right) = \log 6$, which is not true.

The index involving the unknown can be more complicated.

Example

Solve the equation $5^{x-1} = 3^x$.

Solution

In this case, the method of solution is the same, namely taking logs of both sides. This gives

$$\log 5^{x-1} = \log 3^x$$
$$\therefore \quad (x-1)\log 5 = x \log 3$$
$$\therefore \quad x \log 5 - \log 5 = x \log 3$$
$$\therefore \quad x \log 5 - x \log 3 = \log 5$$
$$\therefore \quad x (\log 5 - \log 3) = \log 5$$
$$\therefore \quad x = \frac{\log 5}{\log 5 - \log 3} = 3.151 \ (3\,\text{dp})$$

4 Quadratic equations and functions

An equation of the form $ax^2 + bx + c = 0$, where a, b and c are constants with $a \neq 0$, is called a quadratic equation.

There are three main types of quadratic equation, that you must be able to identify with ease. These are:

- $ax^2 + c = 0$, ($a \neq 0$, $b = 0$, $c \neq 0$)
- $ax^2 + bx = 0$, ($a \neq 0$, $b \neq 0$, $c = 0$)
- $ax^2 + bx + c = 0$, ($a \neq 0$, $b \neq 0$, $c \neq 0$)

The following examples illustrate the methods of solution for each of these types.

Example

Solve the equation $2x^2 - 50 = 0$.

Solution

Rearranging gives

$$2x^2 = 50$$
$$\therefore \quad x^2 = 25$$
$$\therefore \quad x = \pm 5$$

In this case there is an alternative approach, namely to use the factorisation known as 'the difference of two squares'. This gives

$$2(x^2 - 25) = 0$$
$$2(x + 5)(x - 5) = 0$$
$$\therefore \quad x = -5 \text{ or } x = 5$$

Example

Solve the equation $x^2 - 5x = 0$.

Solution

Taking out the factor of x gives

$$x(x - 5) = 0$$

Solving now gives

$$x = 0 \text{ or } x - 5 = 0$$
$$\therefore \quad x = 0 \text{ or } x = 5$$

Example

Solve the equation $x^2 - 3x - 10 = 0$.

Solution
In this case, the LHS needs to be factorised into linear terms, which gives

$$(x + 2)(x - 5) = 0$$

Solving gives

$$x + 2 = 0 \text{ or } x - 5 = 0$$
$$\therefore \quad x = -2 \text{ or } x = 5$$

Note: in the case of this third type, not all quadratics factorise. When this is the case, the quadratic formula is very useful.

4.1 THE QUADRATIC FORMULA

If $ax^2 + bx + c = 0$, where a, b and c are constants with $a \neq 0$, then

$$x = \frac{-b \pm \sqrt{b^2 - 4ac}}{2a}$$

The constant $b^2 - 4ac$ is called the discriminant of the quadratic equation $ax^2 + bx + c = 0$ and is usually denoted by D.

The value of the discriminant provides information about the roots of the quadratic equation:

- if $D > 0$, then the quadratic equation has two real roots
- if $D < 0$, then the quadratic equation has no real roots
- if $D = 0$, then the quadratic equation has one repeated root

Example

Solve the equation $3x^2 + 2x - 2 = 0$.

Solution

In this case, $a = 3$, $b = 2$ and $c = -2$. Substituting into the formula gives

$$x = \frac{-2 \pm \sqrt{2^2 - 4(3)(-2)}}{2(3)}$$

$$= \frac{-2 \pm \sqrt{28}}{6}$$

$$= \frac{-2 \pm 2\sqrt{7}}{6} = \frac{-1 \pm \sqrt{7}}{3}$$

The two roots are $-\frac{1}{3} + \frac{1}{3}\sqrt{7}$ and $-\frac{1}{3} - \frac{1}{3}\sqrt{7}$

In this example, the discriminant is $D = 28 > 0$, i.e. two real roots.

4.2 DISGUISED QUADRATIC EQUATIONS

In some cases, equations do not appear to be quadratic but once manipulated algebraically they can be expressed in the standard quadratic equation form. The following examples illustrate such cases.

Example

Solve the equation $\frac{2}{x} - \frac{2}{x + 1} = 1$.

Solution

To remove the fraction terms, we multiply throughout by $x(x + 1)$, which gives

$$2(x + 1) - 2x = x(x + 1)$$
$$2x + 2 - 2x = x^2 + x$$
$$x^2 + x - 2 = 0$$
$$(x + 2)(x - 1) = 0$$

Solving gives

$$x + 2 = 0 \text{ or } x - 1 = 0$$
$$\therefore \quad x = -2 \text{ or } x = 1$$

Example

Solve the equation $x + 3\sqrt{x} - 28 = 0$.

Solution

Rewriting the equation in the form

$$(x^{\frac{1}{2}})^2 + 3x^{\frac{1}{2}} - 28 = 0$$

shows clearly that this is a quadratic equation in $x^{\frac{1}{2}}$. In other words, by letting $y = x^{\frac{1}{2}}$, we have

$$y^2 + 3y - 28 = 0$$

Factorising in the usual way gives

$$(y - 4)(y + 7) = 0$$

Solving gives

$$y = 4 \text{ or } y = -7$$

In terms of x, this gives

$$x^{\frac{1}{2}} = 4 \text{ or } x^{\frac{1}{2}} = -7$$
$$\therefore \quad x = 16 \text{ or } x = 49$$

4.3 COMPLETING THE SQUARE

This is a process that transforms the standard quadratic expression $ax^2 + bx + c$ into the form

$$a(x + p)^2 + q, \text{ where } p \text{ and } q \text{ are constants.}$$

The process involves finding the constants p and q. When $a = 1$:

- p is found by halving the coefficient of the x term

- q is found by subtracting p^2 from the constant c

This alternative form, $a(x + p)^2 + q$, is used to:

- solve the associated quadratic equation $ax^2 + bx + c = 0$

- extract information about the graph of the quadratic function

Example

Express $x^2 + 2x + 3$ in the form $a(x + p)^2 + q$.

Solution

In this case, $a = 1$. The coefficient of the x term is 2, which gives an integer value of 1 when halved. Completing the square gives

$$x^2 + 2x + 3 = (x + 1)^2 - 1^2 + 3$$
$$= (x + 1)^2 + 2$$

The required form is $(x + 1)^2 + 2$

Example

Express $x^2 + 3x - 1$ in the form $a(x + p)^2 + q$. Hence

(i) solve the equation $x^2 + 3x - 1 = 0$

(ii) sketch the graph of $y = x^2 + 3x - 1$

Solution

In this case, $a = 1$. The coefficient of the x term is 3, which means that we have some fraction terms to deal with. Completing the square gives

$$x^2 + 3x - 1 = \left(x + \frac{3}{2}\right)^2 - \left(\frac{3}{2}\right)^2 - 1$$

$$= \left(x + \frac{3}{2}\right)^2 - \frac{9}{4} - 1$$

$$= \left(x + \frac{3}{2}\right)^2 - \frac{13}{4}$$

The required form is $\left(x + \frac{3}{2}\right)^2 - \frac{13}{4}$

> The question states 'hence', which means that the answer from the first part of the question must be used to answer the second part.

(i) Solving the equation $x^2 + 3x - 1 = 0$ from this form gives

$$x^2 + 3x - 1 = \left(x + \frac{3}{2}\right)^2 - \frac{13}{4} = 0$$

$$\therefore \qquad \left(x + \frac{3}{2}\right)^2 = \frac{13}{4}$$

$$\therefore \qquad x + \frac{3}{2} = \pm\sqrt{\frac{13}{4}} = \pm\frac{\sqrt{13}}{2}$$

$$\therefore \qquad x = \pm\frac{\sqrt{13}}{2} - \frac{3}{2}$$

(ii) To sketch the graph, we return once again to the form

$$y = x^2 + 3x - 1 = \left(x + \frac{3}{2}\right)^2 - \frac{13}{4}$$

The minimum value of y occurs when the squared term is zero. The minimum value of the squared term is zero and this happens when $x = -\frac{3}{2}$.

Therefore, the minimum value of y is $-\frac{13}{4}$.

To summarise, we know that the graph of the function has a minimum turning point $\left(-\frac{3}{2}, -\frac{13}{4}\right)$. We also know that the graph will be symmetrical about the line $x = -\frac{3}{2}$.

The graph of $y = x^2 + 3x - 1$ is shown below.

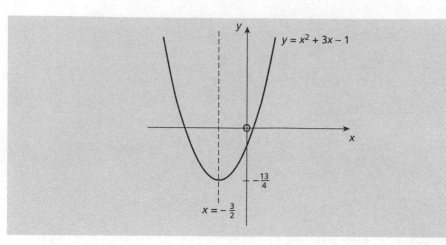

The following example illustrates the technique used for 'completing the square' when $a \neq 1$.

Example

Express $2x^2 + 10x - 1$ in the form $a(x + p)^2 + q$.

Solution

In this case, a factor of 2 is removed, giving

$$2\left(x^2 + 5x - \frac{1}{2}\right)$$

We now 'complete the square' with the quadratic expression inside the bracket, giving

$$2\left(x^2 + 5x - \frac{1}{2}\right) = 2\left(\left(x + \frac{5}{2}\right)^2 - \left(\frac{5}{2}\right)^2 - \frac{1}{2}\right)$$

$$= 2\left(\left(x + \frac{5}{2}\right)^2 - \frac{25}{4} - \frac{1}{2}\right)$$

$$= 2\left(\left(x + \frac{5}{2}\right)^2 - \frac{27}{4}\right)$$

$$= 2\left(x + \frac{5}{2}\right)^2 - \frac{27}{2}$$

The required form is $2\left(x + \frac{5}{2}\right)^2 - \frac{27}{2}$.

Key points

- A quadratic equation takes the general form $ax^2 + bx + c = 0$ $(a \neq 0)$

- A quadratic equation has one of the following:

  - two distinct real roots $(D > 0)$

  - one repeated root $(D = 0)$

  - no real roots $(D < 0)$

- To solve a quadratic equation use:

  - factorisation

- the quadratic formula
- the form $a(x + p)^2 + q$
- The quadratic expression $ax^2 + bx + c$ is transformed into the form $a(x + p)^2 + q$ by the algebraic process called 'completing the square'. This alternative form is used to:
  - find the coordinates of the turning point on the graph of $y = ax^2 + bx + c$ and hence aid in the sketching of the graph
  - solve the quadratic equation $ax^2 + bx + c = 0$

5 Simultaneous equations

5.1 TWO LINEAR

Two linear simultaneous equations can be solved in one of three ways:

- by elimination
- substitution
- graphical methods

The following example illustrates all three methods.

Example

Solve the simultaneous equations

$$x + 3y = 1 \quad (1)$$
$$2x - y = 9 \quad (2)$$

using

(i)   elimination

(ii) substitution

(iii) graphical methods

Solution

(i) *Elimination:* to solve by this method we need to make either the coefficients of the x terms the same or the coefficients of the y terms the same.

The x terms can be made the same by multiplying (1) by 2. This then gives the equations

$$2x + 6y = 2$$
$$2x - y = 9$$

Subtracting now eliminates the x terms and gives

$$7y = -7$$
$$\therefore \qquad y = -1$$

Substituting $y = -1$ into (1) or (2) gives $x = 4$. The solution is $x = 4$, $y = -1$.

(ii) *Substitution*: to solve by this method, we rearrange one of the equations to obtain either y in terms of x or x in terms of y. In this case, it is easier to rearrange (1) for x in terms of y (since the coefficient of x is 1). This gives

$$x = 1 - 3y$$

Substituting for x in (2) gives

$$2(1 - 3y) - y = 9$$

i.e. $\qquad -7y = 7$

$\therefore \qquad\qquad y = -1$

Substituting as before gives $x = 4$.

(iii) *Graphical methods*: to solve by this method we draw the graphs of (1) and (2) and the coordinates of the point of intersection are the solution set of the two equations. The two graphs are shown below

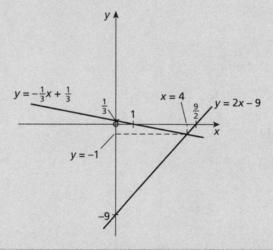

> To sketch the graphs, it is sometimes easier to rearrange each equation into the form $y = mx + c$. In this case, we have $y = -\frac{1}{3}x + \frac{1}{3}$ (1) and $y = 2x - 9$ (2).

From the graph, the coordinates of the intersection point are $x = 4$, $y = -1$, the solution to the simultaneous equations.

5.2 ONE LINEAR AND ONE QUADRATIC

In this case, it is easier to use the algebraic method of substitution to solve the set of equations.

Example

Solve the simultaneous equations

$$y = x^2 - 2x + 3 \qquad (1)$$
$$y = 5x - 3 \qquad (2)$$

Solution

Substituting for y eliminates y and gives

$$x^2 - 2x + 3 = 5x - 3$$
$$\therefore \qquad x^2 - 7x + 6 = 0$$
$$\therefore \qquad (x - 6)(x - 1) = 0$$
$$\therefore \qquad x = 6 \text{ or } x = 1$$

When $x = 6$, $y = 27$. When $x = 1$, $y = 2$. These are the two sets of solutions.

5.3 Two quadratic

In this case, it is easier to use the algebraic method of substitution to solve the set of equations.

Example

Solve the simultaneous equations

$$x^2 + y^2 = 29 \qquad (1)$$
$$y = x^2 + 1 \qquad (2)$$

Solution

Substituting for y from (2) into (1) gives

$$x^2 + (x^2 + 1)^2 = 29$$
i.e. $\qquad x^2 + x^4 + 2x^2 + 1 = 29$
$$x^4 + 3x^2 - 28 = 0$$
$$\therefore \qquad (x^2 - 4)(x^2 + 7) = 0$$
$$\therefore \qquad x^2 - 4 = 0 \text{ or } x^2 + 7 = 0$$

If $x^2 - 4 = 0$ then $x^2 = 4$ and $x = \pm 2$. If $x^2 + 7 = 0$ then this gives no real solutions.

Now, substituting the x values into (2): when $x = 2$, $y = 5$ and when $x = -2$, $y = 5$.

Key points

- There are three methods for solving linear simultaneous equations. These are:
  - elimination
  - substitution
  - graphical
- In the case of (i) one linear, one quadratic and (ii) two quadratic simultaneous equations, use the method substitution method.

6   *Inequalities*

- An inequality is a mathematical statement that involves the use of one of the following inequality symbols:

  $<$ less than $>$ greater than

  $\leq$ less than or equal to $\geq$ greater than or equal to

For example, we would write $3 > 2$.

Inequalities involving unknowns can be simplified in a similar way to equations.

6.1 LINEAR INEQUALITIES

These are inequalities which involve unknowns of at most degree one.

Example

Simplify $2x + 1 < x + 7$.

Solution

Rearranging gives

$$2x - x < 7 - 1$$
$$\therefore \qquad x < 6$$

Therefore, providing that x is less than 6, the original inequality will be satisfied.

An examination question may say 'find the largest positive integer that satisfies $2x + 1 < x + 7$'. In this case, the answer would be 5, since x has to be less than 6.

Important point

When rearranging inequalities, special care has to be taken in one particular case. We know that $3 < 10$ is true. Multiplying both sides by -1 (a technique used frequently when solving equations) gives $-3 < -10$, which is not true.

When multiplying an inequality throughout by -1 the inequality sign must be reversed. The following example illustrates the use of this result.

Example

Simplify $x - 3 \geq 7 + 2x$.

Solution

Rearranging gives

$$-x \geq 10$$
$$\therefore \qquad x \leq -10$$

The inequality sign has been reversed because of multiplying throughout by -1.

6.2 QUADRATIC INEQUALITIES

To solve a quadratic inequality, rearrange into the form

$$ax^2 + bx + c \, \Delta \, 0$$

where Δ represents one of the four inequality symbols. Once in this form, the graph of $y = ax^2 + bx + c$ can be sketched and the inequality solved.

Example

Solve the inequality $x^2 + 4x - 12 \geq 0$.

Solution

This is already in the required form, so we simply need a sketch graph of $y = x^2 + 4x - 12$. Solving the equation $x^2 + 4x - 12 = 0$ tells us where the graph intersects the x-axis. Factorising and solving gives

$$(x + 6)(x - 2) = 0$$
$$\therefore \quad x = -6 \text{ or } x = 2$$

Sketching part of the graph gives

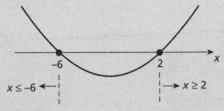

It is now clear for which values of x, $x^2 + 4x - 12 \geq 0$. These are $x \leq -6$ or $x \geq 2$.

6.3 INEQUALITIES AND FRACTIONAL TERMS

When an inequality is multiplied throughout by a constant or algebraic term, the multiplier must be positive. The following example illustrates such a case.

Example

Solve the inequality $\dfrac{x}{x - 1} > 2$.

Solution

This inequality is not in the required quadratic form and involves a fraction. Multiplying throughout by $x - 1$ would simplify the fraction term. However, because this is an inequality, we must make sure that any multiplier is positive. We can do this by multiplying throughout by $(x - 1)^2$.

> A squared term is always positive, as the smallest value it can be is zero.

This gives

$$x(x - 1) > 2(x - 1)^2$$
$$x^2 - x > 2x^2 - 4x + 2$$
$$0 > x^2 - 3x + 2$$

This final line is better written as $x^2 - 3x + 2 < 0$

> Read the final line right to left to see this.

This is now in the required form and the sketch of part of graph of $y = x^2 - 3x + 2$ is shown below.

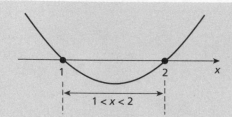

From the graph, the solution is $1 < x < 2$

Key points

- Rearrange the inequality using the same methods as those used to simplify equations remembering the one special case, namely that multiplying throughout by a negative quantity affects the inequality sign.

- In the case of quadratic inequalities, rearrange into the standard form $ax^2 + bx + c \,\Delta\, 0$ and then sketch the graph of $y = ax^2 + bx + c$ and identify the required interval from the x-axis.

- In the case of inequalities that involve fractional terms, multiply throughout by a term that is guaranteed to be positive. For example, if $x + a$ occurs in the denominator then multiply throughout by $(x + a)^2$. Watch out for those cases where the denominator is already positive for all values of x, for example $x^2 + 3$. In these cases multiplying throughout by the denominator term does not cause a problem and squaring of the whole term is not necessary.

7   _Algebraic fractions_

Algebraic fractions can be simplified in a similar way to numerical fractions, namely by finding a common denominator. When identifying the common denominator, it is important to use one that is as simple as possible. In other words, watch out for repeated factors, as illustrated in the second example below.

Example

Simplify $\dfrac{1}{x + 2} + \dfrac{3}{x - 5}$.

Solution

The common denominator is $(x + 2)(x - 5)$, giving

$$\frac{1}{x + 2} + \frac{3}{x - 5} = \frac{(x - 5) + 3(x + 2)}{(x + 2)(x - 5)}$$

$$= \frac{4x + 1}{(x + 2)(x - 5)}$$

Example

Simplify $\dfrac{2x}{x^2 + 2x - 3} - \dfrac{1}{x + 3}$.

Solution

In this case, it is tempting to write $(x^2 + 2x - 3)(x + 3)$ as the common denominator. However, $(x + 3)$ is a factor of $x^2 + 2x - 3$, since $x^2 + 2x - 3 = (x + 3)(x - 1)$. In other words, $(x + 3)$ is a repeated factor. This means that a simpler common denominator is $(x + 3)(x - 1)$, giving

$$\frac{2x}{x^2 + 2x - 3} - \frac{1}{x + 3} = \frac{2x - (x - 1)}{(x + 3)(x - 1)}$$

$$= \frac{x + 1}{(x + 3)(x - 1)}$$

7.1 PARTIAL FRACTIONS

The process of splitting the fraction $\dfrac{4x + 1}{(x + 2)(x - 5)}$ into $\dfrac{1}{x + 2} + \dfrac{3}{x - 5}$ is referred to as 'expressing in partial fractions'.

This process is useful and is used in a number of areas of mathematics, including integration and binomial expansions.

There are four types of algebraic fraction that, once identified, can be expressed in partial fractions: linear, quadratic, repeated and improper.

1 Linear factors

In this case, the denominator contains just linear factors.

Example

Express $\dfrac{4x + 1}{(x + 2)(x - 5)}$ in partial fractions.

Solution

The first step is to assume that $\dfrac{4x + 1}{(x + 2)(x - 5)} = \dfrac{A}{x + 2} + \dfrac{B}{x - 5}$

Multiplying throughout by $(x + 2)(x - 5)$ gives

$$4x + 1 = A(x - 5) + B(x + 2)$$

To find constants A and B,

let $x = 5$: $21 = 7B \Rightarrow B = 3$

let $x = -2$: $-7 = -7A \Rightarrow A = 1$

Therefore,

$$\frac{4x + 1}{(x + 2)(x - 5)} = \frac{1}{x + 2} + \frac{3}{x - 5}$$

2 Quadratic factor

In this case, the denominator contains a quadratic factor that will not factorise into linear terms. If it does, then the first method can be used.

Example

Express $\dfrac{2}{(x + 1)(x^2 + x + 2)}$ in partial fractions.

Solution

Note here that $x^2 + x + 2$ will not factorise into linear factors. The first step is to assume that

$$\frac{2}{(x + 1)\,(x^2 + x + 2)} = \frac{A}{x + 1} + \frac{Bx + C}{x^2 + x + 2}$$

Multiplying throughout by $(x + 1)\,(x^2 + x + 2)$ gives

$$2 = A(x^2 + x + 2) + (Bx + C)\,(x + 1)$$

To find constants A, B and C,

let $x = -1 : 2 = 2A \Rightarrow A = 1$

In this case, the constants B and C cannot be found in this way and the technique of comparing coefficients has to be used. Comparing coefficients of x^2:

$$0 = A + B$$
i.e. $0 = 1 + B \Rightarrow B = -1$

Comparing constants:

$$2 = 2A + C$$
i.e. $2 = 2(1) + C \Rightarrow C = 0$

Therefore,

$$\frac{2}{(x + 1)\,(x^2 + x + 2)} = \frac{1}{x + 1} - \frac{x}{x^2 + x + 2}$$

3 Repeated factor

In this case, the denominator contains a repeated linear factor.

Example

Express $\dfrac{4x^2 + 11}{(x + 2)\,(x - 1)^2}$ in partial fractions.

Solution

The first step is to assume

$$\frac{4x^2 + 11}{(x + 2)\,(x - 1)^2} = \frac{A}{x + 2} + \frac{B}{x - 1} + \frac{C}{(x - 1)^2}$$

Multiplying throughout by $(x + 2)\,(x - 1)^2$ gives

$$4x^2 + 11 = A(x - 1)^2 + B(x + 2)\,(x - 1) + C(x + 2)$$

To find constants A, B and C,

let $x = 1:$ $15 = 3C \Rightarrow C = 5$

let $x = -2:$ $27 = 9A \Rightarrow A = 3$

To find constant B, we need to compare coefficients. Comparing constants:

$$11 = A - 2B + 2C$$

$$-2 = -2B \Rightarrow B = 1$$

$$\therefore \quad \frac{4x^2 + 11}{(x + 2)(x - 1)^2} = \frac{3}{x + 2} + \frac{1}{x - 1} + \frac{5}{(x - 1)^2}$$

4 Improper fractions

In this case, the degree of the numerator is greater than or equal to the degree of the denominator.

Example

Express $\dfrac{x^3 - 2x^2 + 11}{(x - 3)(x + 1)}$ in partial fractions.

Solution

First notice that the degree of the numerator is greater than the degree of the denominator. Since the degree of the numerator is 3 and the degree of the denominator is 2, the quotient after dividing has degree $(3 - 2) = 1$, i.e. it is of the form $Ax + B$.

We assume that

$$\frac{x^3 - 2x^2 + 11}{(x - 3)(x + 1)} = Ax + B + \frac{C}{x - 3} + \frac{D}{x + 1}$$

Multiplying throughout by $(x - 3)(x + 1)$ gives

$$x^3 - 2x^2 + 11 = (Ax + B)(x - 3)(x + 1) + C(x + 1) + D(x - 3)$$

To find constants A, B, C and D,

let $x = 3$: $\qquad 20 = 4C \Rightarrow C = 5$

let $x = -1$: $\qquad 8 = -4D \Rightarrow D = -2$

Comparing coefficients of x^3: $1 = A$

Comparing constants:

$$11 = -3B + C - 3D$$

i.e. $\quad 11 = -3B + 11 \Rightarrow B = 0$

$$\therefore \quad \frac{x^3 - 2x^2 + 11}{(x - 3)(x + 1)} = x + \frac{5}{x - 3} - \frac{2}{x + 1}$$

Key points

- If the degree of the numerator is greater than or equal to the degree of the denominator, then use the method in 4 above. Always do this test first.

- If there is a repeated factor in the denominator, then use the method in 3 above.

- If there is a quadratic factor in the denominator and it will factorise, then use the method in 1 above; if it will not factorise, then use the method in 2 above.

TOPIC 2 Polynomials

1   Basics

An expression of the form

$$a_n x^n + a_{n-1} x^{n-1} + \ldots + a_0$$

where $a_n, a_{n-1} \ldots, a_0$ are real numbers with $a_n \neq 0$ and n a positive integer, is called a **polynomial of degree n**.

For example,

- $x^2 + 3x - 7$ is a polynomial of degree 2. This is called a quadratic.
- $3x^3 + 2x^2 + x + 1$ is a polynomial of degree 3. This is called a cubic.
- $x^3 + 2x^2 + 7x^5 - 2$ is a polynomial of degree 5.

Adding, subtracting and multiplying polynomials gives a polynomial. For example, if $f(x) = x^2 + 3x - 1$ and $g(x) = x^3 + 2x + 1$, then

- $f(x) + g(x) = x^3 + x^2 + 5x$
- $f(x) - g(x) = -x^3 + x^2 + x - 2$
- $f(x)g(x) = (x^2 + 3x - 1)(x^3 + 2x + 1)$
  $$= x^5 + 2x^3 + x^2 + 3x^4 + 6x^2 + 3x - x^3 - 2x - 1$$
  $$= x^5 + 3x^4 + x^3 + 7x^2 + x - 1$$

2   Dividing polynomials

We know that $\frac{7}{2} = 3$ remainder 1. Another way of writing this is $7 = 2 \times 3 + 1$, where 3 is called the quotient and 1 is called the remainder. Similarly, when dividing polynomials there is a quotient and a remainder.

Example

Find the quotient and remainder when $x^2 + 5x + 1$ is divided by $x + 2$.

Writing $x^2 + 5x + 1 = (x + 2)Q + R$, where Q is the quotient and R is the remainder, we see that Q is linear of the form $(x + a)$. Therefore,

$$x^2 + 5x + 1 = (x + 2)(x + a) + R$$
$$= x^2 + x(a + 2) + 2a + R$$

Now, comparing coefficients gives

$$x: \qquad 5 = a + 2 \Rightarrow a = 3$$
$$\text{constants:} \quad 1 = 2a + R \Rightarrow 1 = 6 + R \Rightarrow R = -5$$

Therefore, $x^2 + 5x + 1 = (x + 2)(x + 3) - 5$. The quotient is $(x + 3)$ and the remainder is -5.

2.1 THE REMAINDER THEOREM

When the polynomial $f(x)$ is divided by $(ax - b)$, the remainder is $f\left(\frac{b}{a}\right)$. When $(ax - b)$ is a factor of $f(x)$, the remainder is zero, i.e. $f\left(\frac{b}{a}\right) = 0$. This is a very useful result when factorising polynomials and is called the **factor theorem**.

In the case of the previous example, $f(x) = x^2 + 5x + 1$ and the divisor is $(x + 2)$

i.e. $a = 1, b = -2$

By the remainder theorem, the remainder is $f(-2)$. Now,

$$f(-2) = (-2)^2 + 5(-2) + 1$$
$$= -5$$

The remainder is -5, as expected.

Example

Express the polynomial $f(x) = 2x^3 + x^2 - 13x + 6$ as a product of linear factors. Hence,

(i) solve the equation $f(x) = 0$

(ii) sketch the graph of $y = f(x)$

Solution

If $f(x)$ has a linear factor $ax + b$, the constant b will be a factor of 6, i.e. ± 1, ± 2, ± 3, ± 6.

First, try $f(\pm 1)$, which gives $f(1) = -4$ and $f(-1) = 18$. Therefore, $x \pm 1$ are not factors.

Second, try $f(\pm 2)$, which gives $f(2) = 0$ and $f(-2) = 20$. Since $f(2) = 0$, $x - 2$ is a factor.

Knowing that $(x - 2)$ is a factor, we have

$$2x^3 + x^2 - 13x + 6 = (x - 2)(ax^2 + bx + c)$$

It is clear by inspection that $a = 2$ and $c = -3$. To find b, we compare x coefficients, which gives

$$-13 = c - 2b$$
i.e. $-13 = -3 - 2b$
$\therefore$ $2b = 10$
$\therefore$ $b = 5$

Therefore,

$$2x^3 + x^2 - 13x + 6 = (x - 2)(2x^2 + 5x - 3)$$

Now, factorising $2x^2 + 5x - 3$ gives

$$2x^3 + x^2 - 13x + 6 = (x - 2)(2x - 1)(x + 3)$$

(i) To solve the equation $f(x) = 0$, we write

$$(x - 2)(2x - 1)(x + 3) = 0$$
$$\therefore \quad x - 2 = 0 \text{ or } 2x - 1 = 0 \text{ or } x + 3 = 0$$

Solving gives $x = 2$ or $x = \dfrac{1}{2}$ or $x = -3$

(ii) The roots of $f(x) = 0$ are the x coordinates of the intersection of $y = f(x)$ and the x-axis. The curve crosses the y-axis when $x = 0$, i.e. at $y = 6$. The graph of $y = f(x)$ is shown below.

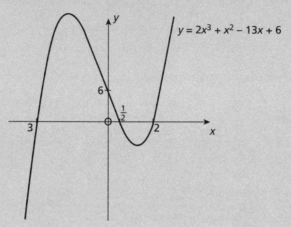

$y = 2x^3 + x^2 - 13x + 6$

TOPIC 3 Functions

1   Notation

Expressions such as $y = x + 5$ can be written using functional notation, i.e. $f(x) = x + 5$. The notation $f(x)$ means a 'function of x'. When we write $f(2)$, we mean the function evaluated when $x = 2$. In the case of $f(x) = x + 5$, we have

$$f(2) = 2 + 5 = 7$$

2   Transformation of the graph of $y = f(x)$

- $f(x) \pm a$ corresponds to a translation of $\pm a$ units parallel to the y-axis, of the graph of $y = f(x)$.

- $f(x \pm a)$ corresponds to a translation of $\mp a$ units parallel to the x-axis, of the graph of $y = f(x)$.

- $f(ax)$ corresponds to a stretch parallel to the x-axis by a scale factor of $\frac{1}{a}$, of the graph of $y = f(x)$.

- $af(x)$ corresponds to a stretch parallel to the y-axis by a scale factor of a, of the graph of $y = f(x)$.

Example

The function f is defined by $f(x) = \frac{1}{x}$, $(x \neq 0)$, where x is a real number. Describe a sequence of geometrical transformations which, when applied to the graph of $y = f(x)$, will give the graph of $g(x) = \frac{2}{x-3}$, $(x \neq 3)$. Sketch the graph of $y = g(x)$.

Solution

The sequence of algebraic transformations and corresponding geometric transformations is

$$f(x) = \frac{1}{x}$$

$$f(x - 3) = \frac{1}{x - 3} \quad \text{(translation of 3 units parallel to } x\text{-axis)}$$

$$2f(x - 3) = \frac{2}{x - 3} \quad \text{(stretch parallel to the } y\text{-axis by a scale factor of 2)}$$

The graph of $y = g(x)$ is shown below.

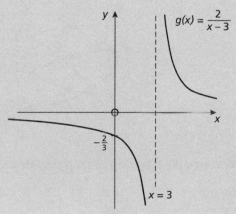

3 Domain, image and range

- The **domain** of a function is the set of permitted x values.

  For example, if $f(x) = \frac{1}{x}$, $x = 0$ is not in the domain of f since it is not permitted. The domain is all real values except $x = 0$.

  > This is a very important point and is something to look out for in examination questions. The function $f(x) = \frac{3}{2x-5}$ is not defined when $x = \frac{5}{2}$. The usual way of writing this is
  >
  > $$f(x) = \frac{3}{2x-5}, x \neq \frac{5}{2}$$

- The **image** is the value of the function for specific x values, i.e. $f(x)$ is called the image of x.

  In the case of $f(x) = x + 5$, we have $f(2) = 7$. The value 7 is the image of 2 under f. On a mapping diagram, we have

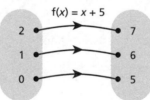

- The **range** of a function is the set of all images.

4 Mappings

In the case of $f(x) = x + 5$, each x value in the domain maps to a distinct image. For example,

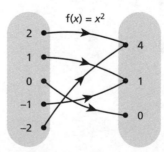

This is called a **one-to-one mapping**.

In the case of $f(x) = x^2$, each x value in the domain does not map to a distinct image, except for 0. For example,

This is called a **two-to-one mapping** or **many-to-one mapping**.

A one-to-one mapping *or* many-to-one mapping is called a **function**. We would only use the word 'function' in such cases.

Example

Determine the range of each of the following functions:

(i) $f(x) = x - 2, \; x \geq 5$

(ii) $f(x) = \dfrac{1}{x}, \; x < -1$

Solution

(i) In this case, the domain is given as $x \geq 5$. Sketching the graph of $f(x) = x - 2$ for $x \geq 5$ enables easy identification of the range:

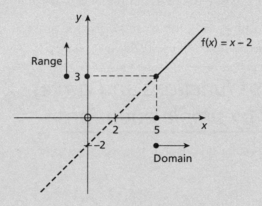

The solid dot indicates that $x = 5$ is included.

The range is $f(x) \geq 3$. (Notice that the 3 is included because $x = 5$ is included.)

(ii) Sketching the graph of $f(x) = \dfrac{1}{x}$ for $x < -1$ gives

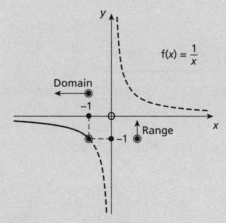

A circled dot indicates that -1 is not included.
The range is $-1 < f(x) < 0$

Key points

- $f(x)$ means a function of x.

- $f(2)$ means the function evaluated when $x = 2$.

- $f(x) \pm a$ corresponds to a translation of $\pm a$ units parallel to the y-axis, of the graph of $y = f(x)$.

- $f(x \pm a)$ corresponds to a translation of $\mp a$ units parallel to the x-axis, of the graph of $y = f(x)$.

- $f(ax)$ corresponds to a stretch parallel to the x-axis by a scale factor of $\frac{1}{a}$, of the graph of $y = f(x)$.

- $af(x)$ corresponds to a stretch parallel to the y-axis by a scale factor of a, of the graph of $y = f(x)$.

- The domain of a function is the set of permitted x values.

- The image of a specific x value is the value of the function evaluated for x.

- The range of a function is the set of all images.

- A function is a one-to-one mapping or a many-to-one mapping.

- To find the range of a function, sketch the graph of $f(x)$ for the given domain and identify the range from the resulting y-values.

5 Graphs of functions and curves defined by simple equations

There are particular graphs that it is essential to know.

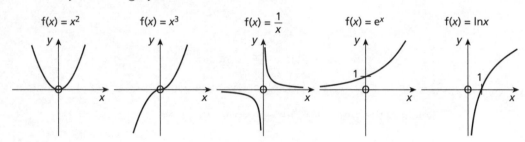

$f(x) = x^2$ $f(x) = x^3$ $f(x) = \frac{1}{x}$ $f(x) = e^x$ $f(x) = \ln x$

6 The modulus function

The modulus function, written as $f(x) = |x|$, is defined as

$$f(x) = |x| = \begin{cases} x, & x \geq 0 \\ -x, & x < 0 \end{cases}$$

In simple terms, $|x|$ means the magnitude of x, i.e. $|-1| = 1 = |+1|$.

The graph of $f(x) = |x|$ is

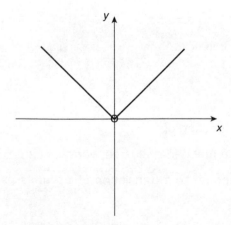

Each line of the graph is at 45° to the horizontal.

6 The modulus function

This graph is derived from the graph of $f(x) = x$ by reflecting the negative part of $f(x) = x$ (that which lies below the x-axis) in the x-axis.

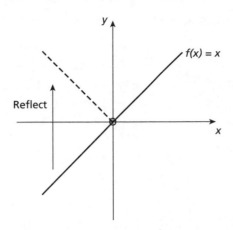

6.1 GRAPHS OF FUNCTIONS INVOLVING MODULUS

Using the same principle, graphs of other functions involving modulus can easily be sketched.

Example

Sketch the graph of $f(x) = |2x + 1|$.

Solution

First, sketch the graph of $f(x) = 2x + 1$ to give

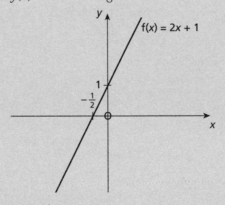

Reflecting the negative part in the x-axis gives

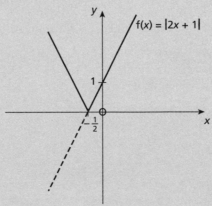

6.2 EQUATIONS AND INEQUALITIES INVOLVING MODULUS

Example

Solve the equation $|x + 7| = 3$.

Solution

Squaring both sides keeps the LHS positive and gives

$$|x + 7|^2 = 3^2$$

The modulus can be ignored because the square ensures that the LHS is positive.

$\therefore \quad (x + 7)(x + 7) = 9$

$\therefore \quad x^2 + 14x + 49 = 9$

$\therefore \quad x^2 + 14x + 40 = 0$

$\therefore \quad (x + 4)(x + 10) = 0$

$\therefore \quad x = -4$ and $x = -10$

Note that the solutions can also be seen by drawing the line $y = 3$ on the same axis as the graph of $f(x) = |x + 7|$:

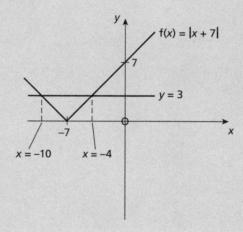

Example

Solve the inequality $|x| > |x - 3|$.

Solution

Squaring both sides keeps both LHS and RHS positive and gives

$$|x|^2 > |x - 3|^2$$

Again, the modulus can be ignored.

$\therefore \quad x^2 > (x - 3)(x - 3)$

$\therefore \quad x^2 > x^2 - 6x + 9$

$\therefore \quad 6x - 9 > 0$

$\therefore \quad x > \dfrac{3}{2}$

The solution set is $x > \dfrac{3}{2}$

Key points

● The modulus function is $f(x) = |x|$.

● To determine the graph of $f(x) = |ax + b|$, sketch $f(x) = ax + b$ and reflect the negative part (that which lies below x-axis) in the x-axis.

● To solve equations or inequalities involving the modulus function, use the 'squaring' technique which ensures everything remains positive.

7 Even, odd and periodic functions

● A function f is called **even** if $f(-x) = f(x)$ for all x belonging to the domain of f.

● The graph of an even function is symmetrical about the y-axis.

● A function f is called **odd** if $f(-x) = -f(x)$ for all x belonging to the domain of f.

● The graph of an odd function has rotational symmetry of $180°$ about the origin.

● A function whose graph repeats itself at regular intervals is called **periodic**. The length of the interval is called the period of the function.

Example

Show that the function $f(x) = x^2 + 3$ is even.

Solution

Now,
$$f(-x) = (-x)^2 + 3$$
$$= x^2 + 3$$
$$= f(x), \text{ which is true for all } x$$

∴ f is even

Note that this can also be seen from the graph of $f(x) = x^2 + 3$, which is symmetrical about the y-axis:

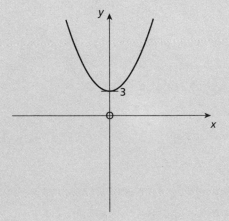

Example

Show that the function $f(x) = \frac{1}{x}$ is odd.

Solution

Now

$$f(-x) = \frac{1}{(-x)}$$
$$= -\frac{1}{x}$$
$$= -f(x), \text{ which is true for all } x$$

∴ f is odd

Note that this can also be seen from the graph of $f(x) = \frac{1}{x}$, which has rotational symmetry of 180° about the origin:

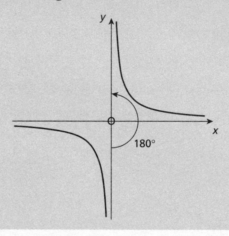

Example

Show that the function $f(x) = \sin x$, is periodic. State the period of f.

Solution

From the graph of $f(x) = \sin x$, we see that f is periodic.

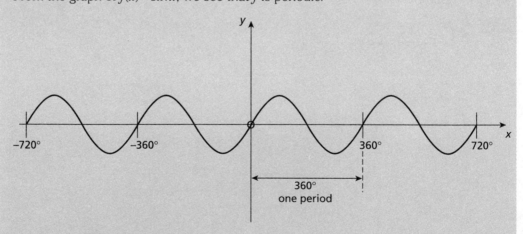

This can also be seen by considering particular x values:

- $f(30°) = f(390°) = f(750°) = 0.5$ etc.

- $f(30°) = f(-330°) = f(-690°) = 0.5$ etc.

The period of f is 360° (or 2π radians).

Example

The function $f(x) = x^2$, $0 < x \leq 1$, is periodic with a period of 1. Sketch the graph of f for $-2 < x \leq 2$.

Solution

The graph of $f(x) = x^2$, $0 < x \leq 1$, is shown below:

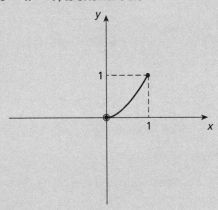

The circled dot at $(0, 0)$ means 'not included' since $0 < x \leq 1$. Since the graph is periodic, with a period of 1, we have

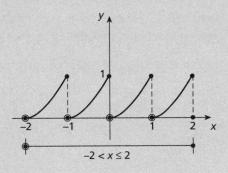

$$-2 < x \leq 2$$

8   *Inverse functions*

Only one-to-one functions have inverses.

A mapping diagram for the function $f(x) = x + 5$ is shown below.

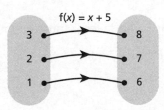

The inverse function, written $f^{-1}(x)$, is the function $f^{-1}(x) = x - 5$ since

$f^{-1}(6) = 6 - 5 = 1$ i.e. back to where it came from

$f^{-1}(7) = 7 - 5 = 2$

$f^{-1}(8) = 8 - 5 = 3$

In this particular case, the function f is a one-to-one function.

Example

The function f is defined by $f(x) = 3x - 2$, where x is a real number. Find $f^{-1}(x)$.

Solution

A useful technique for finding the inverse function is to let $y = f(x)$ and rearrange for x, remembering to change back to variable x.

Let $y = 3x - 2$. Rearranging for x gives

$$3x = y + 2$$

$$\therefore \quad x = \frac{y + 2}{3}$$

Therefore, the inverse function is given by $f^{-1}(x) = \frac{x + 2}{3}$

Important point

The function $y = \ln x$ is one-to-one and has as its inverse the function $y = e^x$.

8.1 RESTRICTING THE DOMAIN OF A FUNCTION

In the case of $f(x) = x^2$, we know that this is not a one-to-one function and therefore does not have an inverse function. However, by restricting the domain of $f(x) = x^2$, a 'different' function can be created that is one-to-one and hence has an inverse.

If we define $f(x) = x^2$, $x \geq 0$, then the graph of this function is

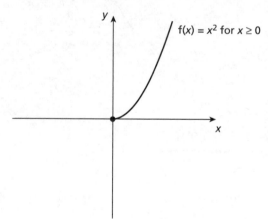

and hence is one-to-one $\Rightarrow$ an inverse function exists.

Using our useful technique for finding $f^{-1}(x)$:

let $y = x^2$

then $x = \pm\sqrt{y}$

Therefore $f^{-1}(x) = +\sqrt{x}$, since we are only considering positive values.

Example

The function f is defined by $f(x) = (x-1)^2$, $x \in R$. Explain why $f^{-1}(x)$ does not exist. By stating a suitable restriction of the domain of f, find $f^{-1}(x)$.

Solution

The graph of $f(x) = (x - 1)^2$ is shown below.

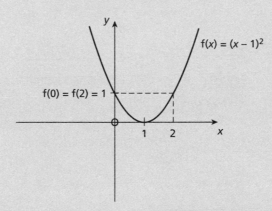

Since $f(0) = f(2) = 1$ the function f is not one-to-one $\Rightarrow f^{-1}$ does not exist.

If we redefine f as $f(x) = (x - 1)^2$, $x \geq 1$, we now have a one-to-one function, which is clear from the graph shown below:

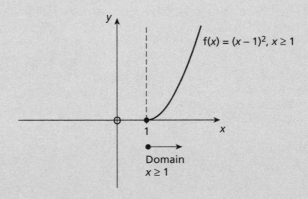

Now f^{-1} exists.

Using our useful technique for finding $f^{-1}(x)$:

$$\text{let } y = (x - 1)^2$$

$$\text{then } (x - 1) = \pm\sqrt{y}$$

$$\therefore \qquad x = 1 \pm \sqrt{y}$$

Therefore, $f^{-1}(x) = 1 + \sqrt{x}$, since we are considering positive values.

8.2 GRAPH OF AN INVERSE FUNCTION

The graph of the inverse function f^{-1} is the reflection of the graph of f in the line $y = x$.

Example

The function f is defined by $f(x) = \dfrac{3}{x - 2}$, where x is a real number, $x \neq 2$. Find $f^{-1}(x)$. Sketch the graph of f and f^{-1}. Find the coordinates of the point of intersection of the two graphs.

Solution

To find $f^{-1}(x)$:

Let $\quad y = \dfrac{3}{x-2}$

$\therefore \quad x - 2 = \dfrac{3}{y}$

$\therefore \quad x = \dfrac{3}{y} + 2$

Therefore, $f^{-1}(x) = \dfrac{3}{x} + 2$, $x \neq 0$.

The graph of $f(x) = \dfrac{3}{x-2}$ is shown below:

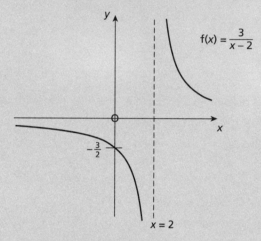

Reflecting in the line $y = x$ gives the graph of f^{-1}:

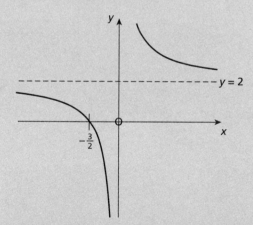

The graphs of f and f^{-1} will intersect at a point on the line $y = x$. Therefore, we need to solve simultaneously $y = x$ and $y = f(x)$ or $y = x$ and $y = f^{-1}(x)$.

Solving $y = x$ and $y = f(x) = \dfrac{3}{x-2}$ gives the equation $x = \dfrac{3}{x-2}$

i.e. $\quad x(x-2) = 3$

$\therefore \quad x^2 - 2x - 3 = 0$

$\therefore \quad (x-3)(x+1) = 0$

$\therefore \quad x = 3$ or $x = -1$

When $x = 3$, $y = 3$. When $x = -1$, $y = -1$.

Therefore, the coordinates of the points of intersection are $(3, 3)$ and $(-1, -1)$.

Important point

The graph of $y = e^x$ is a reflection of the graph of $y = \ln x$ in the line $y = x$, as expected.

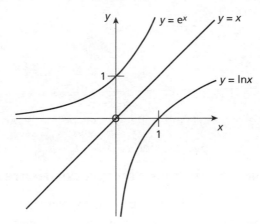

Key points

- Only one-to-one functions have inverses.

- If a function is not one-to-one, restrict the domain to make it one-to-one so that the inverse will exist.

- To find the formula for an inverse function, let $y = f(x)$ and rearrange for x.

- The graph of an inverse function can be obtained by reflecting the graph of the function in the line $y = x$.

- The inverse of the function $y = \ln x$ is the function $y = e^x$.

9 Composite functions

The function $fg(x)$ [also written $f(g(x))$ or $fog(x)$] is called the composite function of f and g. The function g operates first (it is nearest to the x), followed by the function f.

Example

The functions f and g are defined by $f(x) = x + 2$ and $g(x) = 3x - 1$, where x is a real number. Evaluate $fg(2)$ and $gf(2)$.

Solution

In the case of $fg(2)$ the function g operates first so we have

$$fg(2) = f[3(2) - 1]$$
$$= f(5)$$

Now we need to evaluate $f(5)$, which gives

$$f(5) = 5 + 2$$
$$= 7$$
$$\therefore \quad fg(2) = 7$$

In the case of $gf(2)$, the function f operates first so we have

$$gf(2) = g[2 + 2]$$

$$= g(4)$$

$$= 3(4) - 1$$

$$= 11$$

$$\therefore \quad gf(2) = 11$$

Note: this example illustrates that $fg(x)$ is not necessarily the same as $gf(x)$ for all values of x.

9.1 FINDING A FORMULA FOR THE COMPOSITE FUNCTION

Sometimes we only need to evaluate a composite function for a particular value of x (see previous example). In other cases, we need a general formula, in terms of x, for the composite function. In these cases, an algebraic approach is needed. The following example illustrates this approach.

Example

The functions f and g are defined by $f(x) = x + 2$ and $g(x) = 3x - 1$, where x is a real number. Find $fg(x)$ and $gf(x)$.

Solution

$$fg(x) = f[3x - 1]$$
$$= (3x - 1) + 2 \qquad \text{To see this, what does the function } f \text{ do? The function } f \text{ adds 2.}$$
$$= 3x + 1$$
$$\therefore \quad fg(x) = 3x + 1$$
$$gf(x) = g[x + 2]$$
$$= 3(x + 2) - 1 \qquad \text{To see this, what does the function } g \text{ do? The function } g$$
$$= 3x + 6 - 1 \qquad \text{multiplies by 3 and subtracts 1 from the result.}$$
$$= 3x + 5$$
$$\therefore \quad gf(x) = 3x + 5$$

1 | Basics

- The distance d between two points $P(x_1, y_1)$ and $Q(x_2, y_2)$ in the xy-plane is given by

  $$d^2 = (x_2 - x_1)^2 + (y_2 - y_1)^2$$

  i.e. $\quad d = \sqrt{(x_2 - x_1)^2 + (y_2 - y_1)^2}$

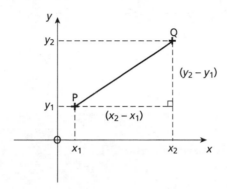

- The coordinates of the mid-point of the straight line joining $P(x_1, y_1)$ and $Q(x_2, y_2)$ are given by

  $$\left(\frac{1}{2}(x_1 + x_2), \frac{1}{2}(y_1 + y_2) \right)$$

- The gradient m of the straight line joining $P(x_1, y_1)$ and $Q(x_2, y_2)$ is given by

  $$m = \frac{y_2 - y_1}{x_2 - x_1}$$

  Note: if the line PQ makes an angle θ with the horizontal, then we have

  $$m = \tan\theta = \frac{y_2 - y_1}{x_2 - x_1}$$

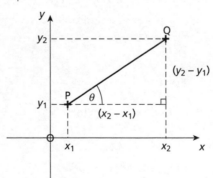

- Parallel lines have the same gradient.

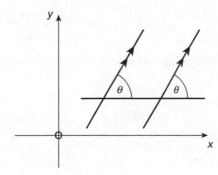

- The product of the gradients of two perpendicular lines is -1.

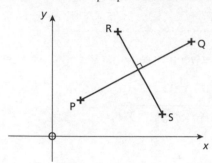

If the gradient of PQ $= m_1$ and the gradient of RS $= m_2$, then $m_1 m_2 = -1$.

Example

A triangle has vertices P(1, 1), Q(5, 9) and R(-1, 7). Find

(i) the length of the sides PR and QR
(ii) the coordinates of the mid-point T, of PQ

Calculate the gradients of lines PQ and RT. Show that PQ and RT are perpendicular.

Solution

(i) Using the distance between two points formula gives

$$\begin{aligned}
\text{PR}^2 &= (-1 - 1)^2 + (7 - 1)^2 \\
&= (-2)^2 + 6^2 \\
&= 40
\end{aligned}$$
$$\therefore \quad \text{PR} = \sqrt{40} = 2\sqrt{10}$$

Using the distance between two points formula again gives

$$\begin{aligned}
\text{QR}^2 &= (-1 - 5)^2 + (7 - 9)^2 \\
&= (-6)^2 + (-2)^2 \\
&= 40
\end{aligned}$$
$$\therefore \quad \text{QR} = \sqrt{40} = 2\sqrt{10}$$

(ii) The mid-point T of PQ has coordinates

$$\left(\tfrac{1}{2}(1 + 5), \tfrac{1}{2}(1 + 9)\right) = (3, 5)$$

The gradient m_1 of PQ is given by

$$m_1 = \frac{9 - 1}{5 - 1} = \frac{8}{4} = 2$$

The gradient m_2 of RT is given by

$$m_2 = \frac{5 - 7}{3 - (-1)} = -\frac{2}{4} = -\frac{1}{2}$$

If PQ and RT are perpendicular then $m_1 \times m_2 = -1$.

Now,

$$m_1 \times m_2 = 2 \times (-\tfrac{1}{2}) = -1$$

Therefore, PQ and RT are perpendicular.

2 *Equation of a straight line*

- The Cartesian form of the equation of a straight line is $y = mx + c$, where m is the gradient and c is the y-intercept.

- The straight line with gradient m passing through the point (x_1, y_1) has equation

$$y - y_1 = m(x - x_1)$$

If we know the gradient (m) and a point (x_1, y_1) that the line passes through then we can find the equation of the line using this result.

Note: the general form for the straight line equation is $ax + by + c = 0$.

Example

Write down the gradient of the straight line with equation $3y - 5x + 9 = 0$.

Solution

Writing this in the form $y = mx + c$ gives

$$3y = 5x - 9$$

$$\therefore \quad y = \frac{5}{3}x - 3$$

The gradient is $\frac{5}{3}$.

Example

Find the equation of the perpendicular bisector of the line PQ, where P and Q have coordinates $(-3, 2)$ and $(5, 6)$ respectively.

Solution

The perpendicular bisector of PQ (i) passes through the mid-point of (i.e. bisects) PQ and (ii) is perpendicular to the line PQ.

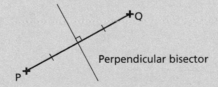

The mid-point of PQ has coordinates

$$\left(\frac{1}{2}(-3 + 5), \frac{1}{2}(2 + 6)\right) = (1, 4)$$

The gradient m_{PQ} of PQ is given by

$$m_{PQ} = \frac{6 - 2}{5 - (-3)} = \frac{4}{8} = \frac{1}{2}$$

Since the perpendicular bisector is perpendicular to PQ, it has gradient

$$-\frac{1}{m_{PQ}} = -\frac{1}{\left(\frac{1}{2}\right)} = -2$$

We know (i) a point that the line passes through and (ii) the gradient. Therefore, we can find the equation of the straight line.

Using $y - y_1 = m(x - x_1)$ gives

$$y - 4 = -2(x - 1)$$
$$\therefore \qquad y = -2x + 2 + 4$$
$$\therefore \qquad y = -2x + 6$$
$$\therefore \qquad 2x + y - 6 = 0$$

3 Distance of a point from a line

The perpendicular distance of (x_1, y_1) from the line $ax + by + c = 0$ is given by

$$\left| \frac{ax_1 + by_1 + c}{\sqrt{a^2 + b^2}} \right|$$

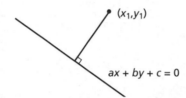

Example

Find the distance of the point $(1, 2)$ from the line $y = 5x - 1$.

Solution

To use the formula given above, we must identify the constants a, b and c.

Rearranging $y = 5x - 1$ into the form $5x - y - 1 = 0$, gives $a = 5$, $b = -1$ and $c = -1$. Therefore, the required distance d is given by

$$d = \left| \frac{5(1) + (-1)(2) + (-1)}{\sqrt{(5)^2 + (-1)^2}} \right|$$

$$\therefore \qquad d = \left| \frac{2}{\sqrt{26}} \right|$$

$$\therefore \qquad d = \frac{2}{\sqrt{26}}$$

The required distance is $\dfrac{2}{\sqrt{26}}$.

4 Angle between two lines

The angle θ between the two lines $y = m_1 x + c_1$ and $y = m_2 x + c_2$ is given by

$$\theta = \tan^{-1}\left(\frac{m_1 - m_2}{1 + m_1 m_2} \right)$$

Example

Find the acute angle between the two lines $y = 2x - 3$ and $y - x - 3 = 0$.

Solution

We need the gradient of each line.

The line $y = 2x - 3$ has gradient 2.

The line $y - x - 3 = 0$ can be expressed in the form $y = x + 3$ and therefore the gradient is 1.

Letting $m_1 = 2$ and $m_2 = 1$, the angle θ between the two lines is given by

$$\theta = \tan^{-1}\left(\frac{2 - 1}{1 + (2)(1)}\right)$$

$$\therefore \quad \theta = \tan^{-1}\left(\frac{1}{3}\right)$$

$$\therefore \quad \theta = 18.4° \text{ (1 dp)}$$

The acute angle between the lines is 18.4°.

5 The circle

- A circle with centre (0, 0) and radius r has equation $x^2 + y^2 = r^2$.

- A circle with centre (a, b) and radius r has equation $(x - a)^2 + (y - b)^2 = r^2$.

The following example illustrates how to find the equation of a circle given the centre and the radius.

Example

Find the equation of the circle with centre $(3, -5)$ and radius 2.

Solution

The equation is

$$(x - 3)^2 + (y - (-5))^2 = 2^2$$

i.e. $\qquad (x - 3)^2 + (y + 5)^2 = 4$

An alternative form is obtained by expanding and simplifying. This gives

$$x^2 - 6x + 9 + y^2 + 10y + 25 = 4$$

i.e. $\qquad x^2 + y^2 - 6x + 10y + 30 = 0$

> This alternative form is written with terms in a particular order, i.e. x^2 and y^2 terms first, x and y terms second and then, third, the constant.

The following example illustrates how to find the centre and radius, given the equation of a circle.

Example

Find the centre and radius of the circle $x^2 + y^2 - 2x + 8y + 8 = 0$.

Solution

We aim to write the circle equation in the form $(x-a)^2 + (y-b)^2 = r^2$, since (a, b) will be the centre and r the radius.

To do this, we rearrange the equation and complete the square for both x and y. This gives

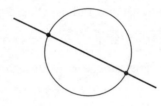

$$x^2 - 2x + y^2 + 8y + 8 = 0$$
i.e. $\quad (x-1)^2 - 1 + (y+4)^2 - 16 + 8 = 0$
$\therefore \qquad\qquad\qquad (x-1)^2 + (y+4)^2 - 9 = 0$
$\therefore \qquad\qquad\qquad (x-1)^2 + (y-(-4))^2 = 3^2$

Therefore, the centre is $(1, -4)$ and the radius is 3.

5.1 INTERSECTION OF A LINE AND A CIRCLE

Consider the straight line $y = mx + c$ and the circle $(x - a)^2 + (y - b)^2 = r^2$. There are three possible cases to consider.

1 The line intersects the circle at two distinct points.

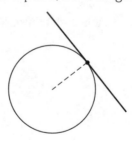

2 The line touches the circle at one point, i.e. a tangent to the circle.

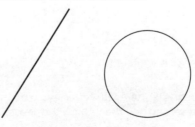

3 The line does not intersect or touch the circle.

Each case is determined by solving, simultaneously, the equations $y = mx + c$ and $(x - a)^2 + (y - b)^2 = r^2$. If the resulting quadratic equation has

- two distinct real roots, then case 1 applies

- one repeated real root, then case 2 applies

- no real roots, then case 3 applies

Example

Show that the line $x + 6y - 7 = 0$ touches the circle $x^2 + y^2 - x + 4y - 5 = 0$.

Solution

Now, $x = 7 - 6y$. Substituting into the circle equation gives

$$(7 - 6y)^2 + y^2 - (7 - 6y) + 4y - 5 = 0$$
$$\therefore \quad 49 - 84y + 36y^2 + y^2 - 7 + 6y + 4y - 5 = 0$$
$$\therefore \quad 37y^2 - 74y + 37 = 0$$
$$\therefore \quad 37(y^2 - 2y + 1) = 0$$
$$\therefore \quad 37(y - 1)^2 = 0$$
$$\therefore \quad y = 1$$

i.e. a repeated root, as expected for this case.

When $y = 1$, $x = 7 - 6(1) = 1$.

Therefore, the line $x + 6y - 7 = 0$ touches the circle $x^2 + y^2 - x + 4y - 5 = 0$ at the point $(1, 1)$.

6 Parametric equations of curves

In some cases, a function is defined by expressing both y and x in terms of a third variable, usually t. This third variable is known as a parameter. Such equations are called **parametric equations**.

Examples of parametric equations:

$$x = t + 1, y = t^2 - 3$$
$$x = \frac{1}{t - 1}, y = \frac{t}{t + 1}$$
$$x = \sin t, y = \cos t$$
$$x = e^{2t}, y = e^t$$

6.1 SKETCHING A CURVE FROM THE PARAMETRIC FORM

A range of values for the parameter will give a number of coordinates of points on the curve.

Example

Sketch the curve defined by $x = t^2$, $y = t^3$ for $-3 \leq t \leq 3$.

Solution

Completing a table of values for $-3 \leq t \leq 3$ gives

t	-3	-2	-1	0	1	2	3
x	9	4	1	0	1	4	9
y	-27	-8	-1	0	1	8	27

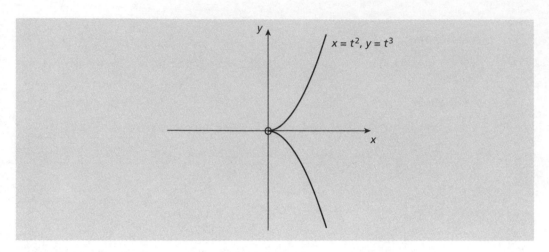

6.2 DETERMINING THE CARTESIAN FORM

Given the parametric form of a curve, eliminating the parameter will give the Cartesian form.

Example

Find the Cartesian equation for each of the following parametric forms:

(i) $x = t - 1, y = \dfrac{2}{t + 1}$

(ii) $x = 2\sin t, y = \cos t$

Solution

(i) If $x = t - 1$ then $t = x + 1$. Substituting into $y = \dfrac{2}{t + 1}$ gives

$$y = \frac{2}{(x + 1) + 1}$$

$\therefore \quad y = \dfrac{2}{x + 2}$, the required Cartesian equation.

(ii) If $x = 2\sin t$ then $x^2 = 4\sin^2 t$. If $y = \cos t$ then $y^2 = \cos^2 t$.

Now, $\sin^2 t + \cos^2 t = 1$, therefore

$$\frac{x^2}{4} + y^2 = 1$$

$\therefore \quad x^2 + 4y^2 = 4$, the required Cartesian equation

7 Curve sketching

There are a number of 'standard' curves that you should know, some of which appear elsewhere in this book. These are:

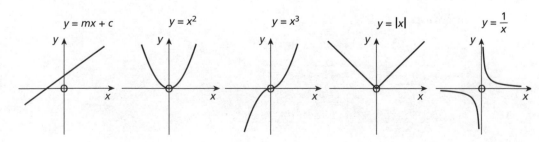

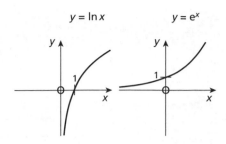

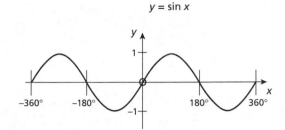

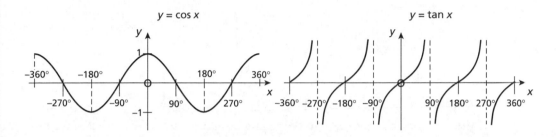

7.1 GRAPHS OF RATIONAL FUNCTIONS

- $y = \dfrac{ax + b}{cx + d}$

These functions are not defined for all x.

Example

Sketch the curve $y = \dfrac{x + 1}{2x + 1}$.

Solution

First, consider intersections with axes:

when $x = 0$, $y = 1$

when $y = 0$, $x = -1$

Second, notice that y is not defined when $2x + 1 = 0$, i.e. $x = -\dfrac{1}{2}$.

To determine when x is not defined, rearrange for x. This gives

$$y(2x + 1) = x + 1$$

$$\therefore \quad 2xy + y = x + 1$$

$$\therefore \quad 2xy - x = 1 - y$$

$$\therefore \quad x(2y - 1) = 1 - y$$

$$\therefore \quad x = \dfrac{1 - y}{2y - 1}$$

Therefore, x is not defined when $y = \dfrac{1}{2}$.

We have enough information to sketch the curve.

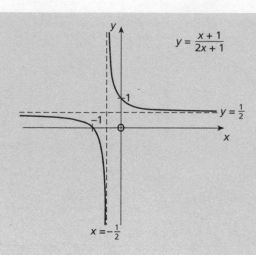

$$y = \frac{x+1}{2x+1}$$

Note: the lines $x = -\frac{1}{2}$ and $y = \frac{1}{2}$ are called *asymptotes*, since the curve approaches them more and more closely. For example, as $x \to +\infty$ the curve approaches $y = \frac{1}{2}$ from the positive side. As $x \to -\infty$ the curve approaches $y = \frac{1}{2}$ from the negative side.

- $y = \dfrac{ax^2 + bx + c}{dx^2 + ex + f}$

In this case, the curve may possess turning points due to the quadratic terms. Therefore, a more detailed analysis is needed than that in (i) above.

A suggested approach is as follows:

- determine intersections with axes (I)

- determine where y is not defined (N)

- determine where x is not defined (N)

- determine turning points (T)

- determine asymptotes (A)

You can remember this as INTA:

    I = intersections

    N = not defined

    T = turning points

    A = asymptotes

Example

Sketch the curve $y = \dfrac{x}{x^2 + 1}$.

Solution

Intersections: when $x = 0, y = 0$

Not defined: y is defined for all x values, since $x^2 + 1 \neq 0$

To determine when x is not defined, rearrange for x, which gives

$$y(x^2 + 1) = x$$

$$\therefore \quad yx^2 - x + y = 0$$

This is a quadratic in x. Using the quadratic formula gives

$$x = \frac{-(-1) \pm \sqrt{(-1)^2 - 4(y)\,(y)}}{2y}$$

$$\therefore \quad x = \frac{1 \pm \sqrt{1 - 4y^2}}{2y}$$

Now, x is defined providing $1 - 4y^2$ (the discriminant) is zero or positive. Therefore, x is not defined when

$$1 - 4y^2 < 0$$

i.e. $\quad (1 - 2y)(1 + 2y) < 0$

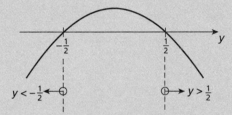

$$\therefore \quad y < -\frac{1}{2} \text{ or } y > \frac{1}{2}$$

Turning points: using the quotient rule to find $\dfrac{dy}{dx}$ gives

$$\frac{dy}{dx} = \frac{(x^2 + 1)\,1 - x\,(2x)}{(x^2 + 1)^2}$$

$$\therefore \quad \frac{dy}{dx} = \frac{x^2 + 1 - 2x^2}{(x^2 + 1)^2}$$

$$\therefore \quad \frac{dy}{dx} = \frac{1 - x^2}{(x^2 + 1)^2}$$

Turning points occur when $\dfrac{dy}{dx} = 0$

i.e. $\quad 1 - x^2 = 0$

$$\therefore \quad x = 1 \text{ or } x = -1$$

When $x = 1$, $y = \dfrac{1}{1^2 + 1} = \dfrac{1}{2}$

When $x = -1$, $y = \dfrac{-1}{(-1)^2 + 1} = -\dfrac{1}{2}$

Asymptotes: As $x \to +\infty$, $y \to 0$ from the positive side

As $x \to -\infty$, $y \to 0$ from the negative side

The sketch is shown below:

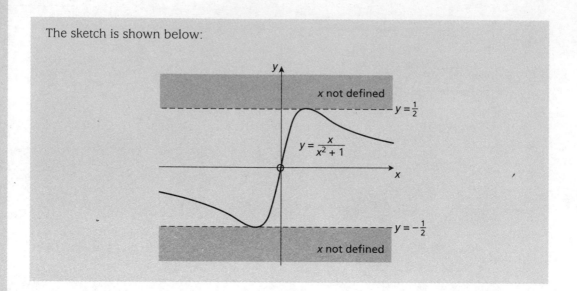

1 Sequences

A **sequence** is a set of numbers derived from a particular rule. For example, the rule

$$n\text{th term} = x_n = 2n + 1$$

generates the sequence

$$1, 3, 5, 7, \ldots \text{ for } n \geq 0$$

A sequence can be defined by a recurrence relation, which has the general form $x_{n+1} = f(x_n)$. In other words, the general term x_{n+1} is defined in terms of the previous term of the sequence, namely x_n. For example,

$$x_{n+1} = 3x_n - 2$$

Example

A sequence is defined by $x_{n+1} = x_n - 3$, where the first term is $x_1 = -2$. Write down the first three terms of the sequence.

Solution

Using the recurrence relation $x_{n+1} = x_n - 3$ gives

$$x_2 = x_1 - 3$$

$$\therefore \quad x_2 = -2 - 3 = -5$$

Using it a second time gives

$$x_3 = x_2 - 3$$

$$\therefore \quad x_3 = -5 - 3 = -8$$

The first three terms of the sequence are $-2, -5, -8$.

1.1 CHARACTERISTICS OF SEQUENCES

Sequences can be convergent, divergent, oscillating or periodic. An example of each is shown below.

Example

Write down the first five terms of each of the following sequences and describe the behaviour of the sequence.

(i) $x_n = \dfrac{n}{n + 1}, n \geq 1$

(ii) $x_n = n\cos n, n \geq 1$

(iii) $x_{n+1} = 3 - x_n, x_1 = 2$

(iv) $x_{n+1} = 5 - 3x_n, x_1 = 3$

Solution

(i) $x_n = \dfrac{n}{n-1}$ gives the sequence $\dfrac{1}{2}, \dfrac{2}{3}, \dfrac{3}{4}, \dfrac{4}{5}, \dfrac{5}{6}$

The sequence is converging to 1.

(ii) $x_n = n\cos n$ gives the sequence $0.5403, -0.8323, -2.9700, -2.6146, 1.4183$

The sequence is oscillating.

(iii) $x_{n+1} = 3 - x_n$, $x_1 = 2$ gives the sequence 2, 1, 2, 1, 2

The sequence is periodic, of period 2.

(iv) $x_{n+1} = 5 - 3x_n$, $x_1 = 3$ gives the sequence 3, -4, 17, -46, 143

The sequence is divergent.

2 Series

A **series** is the sum of a number of terms of a sequence. Using sigma ($\sum$) notation we write the sum S_n as

$$S_n = x_1 + x_2 + \ldots + x_n = \sum_{r=1}^{n} x_r$$

Certain series can be summed by using the results:

$$1 + 2 + \ldots + n = \sum_{r=1}^{n} r = \frac{n}{2}(n+1)$$

$$1^2 + 2^2 + \ldots + n^2 = \sum_{r=1}^{n} r^2 = \frac{n}{6}(n+1)(2n+1)$$

$$1^3 + 2^3 + \ldots + n^3 = \sum_{r=1}^{n} r^3 = \frac{n^2}{4}(n+1)^2$$

Example

Find

(i) $\displaystyle\sum_{r=1}^{2n-1} r$

(ii) $\displaystyle\sum_{r=1}^{n} (2r)^3$

Solution

(i) Now,

$$\sum_{r=1}^{2n-1} r = \frac{(2n-1)}{2}\{(2n-1) + 1\}$$

$$= \frac{(2n-1)}{2}(2n)$$

$$= n(2n-1)$$

(ii) Now,

$$\sum_{r=1}^{n} (2r)^3 = 8\sum_{r=1}^{n} r^3 = \frac{8n^2}{4}(n+1)^2 = 2n^2(n+1)^2$$

3 Arithmetic progressions (APs)

- An **arithmetic progression** is a sequence of numbers in which any term can be obtained from the previous term by adding a common difference.

- The **first term** is denoted by a.

- The **common difference** is denoted by d.

- The terms of an AP:

$$a, a + d, a + 2d, \ldots a + (n-1)d, \ldots$$

where $a + (n-1)d$ is the nth term.

- The sum of the first n terms of an AP is given by

$$S_n = \frac{n}{2}(2a + (n-1)d)$$

Example

In an AP, the sum of the first ten terms is 255 and the common difference is 5. Find the first term.

Solution

We have

$$S_{10} = 255 \text{ and } d = 5$$
$$\therefore \quad 255 = \frac{10}{2}(2a + (10-1)\,5)$$
$$\therefore \quad 255 = 5(2a + 45)$$
$$\therefore \quad 2a + 45 = 51$$
$$\therefore \quad 2a = 6$$
$$\therefore \quad a = 3$$

The first term is 3.

4 Geometric progressions (GPs)

- A **geometric progression** is a sequence of numbers in which any term can be obtained from the previous term by multiplying by a common ratio.

- The **first term** is denoted by a.

- The **common ratio** is denoted by r.

- The terms of a GP:

$$a, ar, ar^2, \ldots ar^{n-1}, \ldots$$

where ar^{n-1} is the nth term.

- The sum of the first n terms of a GP is given by

$$S_n = a\left(\frac{r^n - 1}{r - 1}\right) = a\left(\frac{1 - r^n}{1 - r}\right)$$

Example

The sum of the first and third terms of a GP is 20. The sum of the fifth and seventh terms is 320. Find the possible values of the common ratio and the corresponding first term.

Solution

We have 1st term $= a$, 3rd term $= ar^2$, 5th term $= ar^4$, 7th term $= ar^6$. Therefore

$$a + ar^2 = 20$$
$$\therefore \quad a(1 + r^2) = 20 \qquad (1)$$

and

$$ar^4 + ar^6 = 320$$
$$\therefore \quad ar^4(1 + r^2) = 320 \qquad (2)$$

From (2)

$$r^4 = \frac{320}{a(1 + r^2)}$$

Substituting from (1) gives

$$r^4 = \frac{320}{20} = 16$$
$$\therefore \quad r^4 - 16 = 0$$
$$(r^2 - 4)(r^2 + 4) = 0$$
$$\therefore \quad r = \pm 2$$

The possible common ratios are 2 and -2.

The first term is given by

$$a = \frac{20}{1 + r^2}$$
$$\therefore \quad a = \frac{20}{1 + 4} = 4$$

The first term is 4.

4.1 Infinite GPs

- When the common ratio r is such that $-1 < r < 1$, then the 'sum to infinity' S_∞ of the corresponding GP exists.

- The sum to infinity of a GP is given by

$$S_\infty = \frac{a}{1 - r}, \text{ where } -1 < r < 1$$

Example

Find $\sum_{r=1}^{\infty} (0.2)^r$.

Solution

We have $\sum_{r=1}^{\infty} (0.2)^r = 0.2 + (0.2)^2 + \dots$

This is a GP with $a = 0.2$ and $r = 0.2$. The sum to infinity is given by

$$S_\infty = \frac{a}{1 - r} = \frac{0.2}{1 - 0.2} = 0.25$$
$$\therefore \quad \sum_{r=1}^{\infty} (0.2)^r = 0.25$$

TOPIC 6 Binomial expansions

1 Binomial expansion of $(1 + x)^n$, for positive integer n

We know that $(1 + x)^2$ can be expanded and simplified to give $1 + 2x + x^2$. The binomial expansion enables the expansion of $(1 + x)^n$ to be written down directly without having to go through all the intermediate simplifying steps. This is given by

$$(1 + x)^n = 1 + \binom{n}{1}x + \binom{n}{2}x^2 + \ldots + x^n$$

where $\binom{n}{r} = \dfrac{n!}{r!(n - r)!}$

(Remember that $0! = 1$ by definition.)

Note: some calculators have a key marked ^nC_r, which is equal to $\binom{n}{r}$.

This expansion is sometimes written in the form

$$(1 + x)^n = \sum_{r=0}^{n}\binom{n}{r}x^r$$

Another form of this expansion is

$$(1 + x)^n = 1 + nx + \frac{n(n - 1)}{2!}x^2 + \frac{n(n - 1)(n - 2)}{3!}x^3 + \ldots + x^n$$

Example

Write down the expansion of $(1 + x)^5$.

Solution

Using the expansion above and the calculator key ^nC_r gives

$$(1 + x)^5 = 1 + \binom{5}{1}x + \binom{5}{2}x^2 + \binom{5}{3}x^3 + \binom{5}{4}x^4 + \binom{5}{5}x^5$$

$$= 1 + 5x + 10x^2 + 10x^3 + 5x^4 + x^5$$

Without the calculator key,

$$(1 + x)^5 = 1 + 5x + \frac{5(5 - 1)}{2!}x^2 + \frac{5(5 - 1)(5 - 2)}{3!}x^3 + \frac{5(5 - 1)(5 - 2)(5 - 3)}{4!}x^4 + x^5$$

$$= 1 + 5x + 10x^2 + 10x^3 + 5x^4 + x^5$$

Example

Write down the expansion of $(1 + 2x)^4$.

Solution

$$(1 + 2x)^4 = 1 + \binom{4}{1}(2x) + \binom{4}{2}(2x)^2 + \binom{4}{3}(2x)^3 + (2x)^4$$

$$= 1 + 8x + 24x^2 + 32x^3 + 16x^4$$

2 Binomial expansion of (a + b)ⁿ, for positive integer n

In this case, the binomial expansion is

$$(a + b)^n = a^n + \binom{n}{1} a^{n-1}b + \binom{n}{2} a^{n-2}b^2 + \binom{n}{3} a^{n-3}b^3 + \ldots + b^n$$

Example

Expand $(3 - x)^4$ in powers of x.

Solution

Using the form given above gives

$$(3 + (-x))^4 = 3^4 + \binom{4}{1} 3^3(-x) + \binom{4}{2} 3^2(-x)^2 + \binom{4}{3} 3^1(-x)^3 + (-x)^4$$

$$= 81 - 108x + 54x^2 - 12x^3 + x^4$$

An alternative method is to remove a factor of 3 and then use the expansion form for $(1 + x)^n$. This method is illustrated below.

$$\left\{ 3 \left(1 - \frac{x}{3} \right) \right\}^4 = 3^4 \left(1 + \left(\frac{-x}{3} \right) \right)^4$$

Expanding $\left(1 + \left(\frac{-x}{3} \right) \right)^4$ gives

$$\left(1 + \left(\frac{-x}{3} \right) \right)^4 = 1 + \binom{4}{1}\left(\frac{-x}{3} \right) + \binom{4}{2}\left(\frac{-x}{3} \right)^2 + \binom{4}{3}\left(\frac{-x}{3} \right)^3 + \left(\frac{-x}{3} \right)^4$$

$$= 1 - \frac{4}{3}x + \frac{6}{9}x^2 - \frac{4}{27}x^3 + \frac{1}{81}x^4$$

Therefore

$$3^4 \left(1 + \left(\frac{-x}{3} \right) \right)^4 = 81\left(1 - \frac{4}{3}x + \frac{6}{9}x^2 - \frac{4}{27}x^3 + \frac{1}{81}x^4 \right)$$

$$= 81 - 108x + 54x^2 - 12x^3 + x^4$$

as before.

3 Binomial expansion of (1 + x)ⁿ, when n is not a positive integer

In this case, the expansion

$$(1 + x)^n = 1 + nx + \frac{n(n - 1)}{2!}x^2 + \frac{n(n - 1)(n - 2)}{3!}x^3 + \ldots$$

does not terminate and is only valid for $-1 < x < 1$, i.e. $|x| < 1$.

This expansion gives an approximation to $(1 + x)^n$ for $|x| < 1$. The approximation becomes more accurate the more terms that are taken.

Example

Obtain the first three terms in the series expansion of $\dfrac{1}{(1+x)^2}$.

Solution

We have $\dfrac{1}{(1+x)^2} = (1+x)^{-2}$ and the binomial expansion gives

$$(1+x)^{-2} = 1 + (-2)x + \frac{(-2)(-2-1)}{2!}x^2 + \ldots$$

$$= 1 - 2x + 3x^2 + \ldots$$

Therefore,

$$(1+x)^{-2} \approx 1 - 2x + 3x^2, \text{ valid for } |x| < 1$$

Note: some examination questions ask for a decimal approximation of a rational number, derived by substituting for x within the valid range. For example, by letting $x = \frac{1}{3}$ in the expansion derived above, a decimal approximation of $\frac{9}{16}$ can be obtained.

We have

$$\frac{1}{(1+x)^2} \approx 1 - 2x + 3x^2 \text{ for } |x| < 1$$

If $x = \frac{1}{3}$ then

$$\frac{1}{\left(1+\frac{1}{3}\right)^2} \approx 1 - 2\left(\frac{1}{3}\right) + 3\left(\frac{1}{3}\right)^2$$

(Valid, since $\left|\frac{1}{3}\right| < 1$)

i.e. $\dfrac{1}{\left(\frac{16}{9}\right)} \approx 0.67$ (2 dp)

i.e. $\dfrac{9}{16} \approx 0.67$

Since $\frac{9}{16} = 0.5625$, we see that this is a poor approximation. The approximation would be better if more than three terms had been used.

Example

Given that x is small, write down a cubic approximation of $\dfrac{1-x}{\sqrt{1+2x}}$, stating the range of values of x for which the approximation is valid.

By letting $x = \frac{1}{4}$, show that $\sqrt{6} \approx \frac{19}{8}$.

Solution

We have $\dfrac{1-x}{\sqrt{1+2x}} = (1-x)(1+2x)^{-\frac{1}{2}}$

Expanding $(1+2x)^{-\frac{1}{2}}$ gives

$$(1+2x)^{-\frac{1}{2}} = 1 + \left(-\frac{1}{2}\right)(2x) + \frac{\left(-\frac{1}{2}\right)\left(-\frac{1}{2}-1\right)}{2!}(2x)^2 + \frac{\left(-\frac{1}{2}\right)\left(-\frac{1}{2}-1\right)\left(-\frac{1}{2}-2\right)}{3!}(2x)^3$$

$$= 1 - x + \frac{3}{2}x^2 - \frac{5}{2}x^3 + \ldots$$

Therefore,

$$(1-x)(1+2x)^{-\frac{1}{2}} = (1-x)\left(1 - x + \frac{3}{2}x^2 - \frac{5}{2}x^3 + \dots\right)$$

$$= 1 - x + \frac{3}{2}x^2 - \frac{5}{2}x^3 + \dots - x + x^2 - \frac{3}{2}x^3 + \dots$$

$$\approx 1 - 2x + \frac{5}{2}x^2 - 4x^3$$

This approximation is valid for $-1 < 2x < 1$, i.e. $-\frac{1}{2} < x < \frac{1}{2}$ or $|x| < \frac{1}{2}$.

If $x = \frac{1}{4}$, then the above expansion is valid since $\left|\frac{1}{4}\right| < \frac{1}{2}$.

Substituting gives

$$\frac{\left(1 - \frac{1}{4}\right)}{\sqrt{1 + 2\left(\frac{1}{4}\right)}} \approx 1 - 2\left(\frac{1}{4}\right) + \frac{5}{2}\left(\frac{1}{4}\right)^2 - 4\left(\frac{1}{4}\right)^3$$

$$\therefore \quad \frac{\left(\frac{3}{4}\right)}{\sqrt{\frac{6}{4}}} \approx \frac{19}{32}$$

$$\therefore \quad \left(\frac{3}{4}\right) \times \frac{2}{\sqrt{6}} \approx \frac{19}{32}$$

$$\therefore \quad \frac{3}{2\sqrt{6}} \times \frac{\sqrt{6}}{\sqrt{6}} \approx \frac{19}{32}$$

$$\therefore \quad \frac{\sqrt{6}}{4} \approx \frac{19}{32}$$

$$\therefore \quad \sqrt{6} \approx \frac{19}{8}, \text{ as required}$$

4 Use of partial fractions to obtain series expansions

The following example illustrates how partial fractions can be used to split an algebraic fraction, and then how the use of the binomial expansion gives the series expansion.

Example

Express $\frac{5 + 2x}{(1 + x)(2 - x)}$ in partial fractions and hence obtain the series expansion up to and including the term in x^3. State the range of values of x for which the expansion is valid.

Solution

Using partial fraction techniques,

$$\frac{5 + 2x}{(1 + x)(2 - x)} = \frac{A}{1 + x} + \frac{B}{2 - x}$$

gives

$$\frac{5 + 2x}{(1 + x)(2 - x)} = \frac{1}{1 + x} + \frac{3}{2 - x}$$

We now need the expansion of both $\dfrac{1}{1+x}$ and $\dfrac{3}{2-x}$.

Now,

$$\frac{1}{1+x} = (1+x)^{-1}$$

Using the appropriate binomial expansion, gives

$$(1+x)^{-1} = 1 + (-1)x + \frac{(-1)(-1-1)}{2!}x^2 + \frac{(-1)(-1-1)(-1-2)}{3!}x^3 + \ldots$$

$$= 1 - x + x^2 - x^3 + \ldots$$

This expansion is valid for $-1 < x < 1$.

Now,

$$\frac{3}{2-x} = 3(2-x)^{-1} = 3\left(2\left(1-\frac{x}{2}\right)\right)^{-1} = \frac{3}{2}\left(1-\frac{x}{2}\right)^{-1}$$

Using the appropriate binomial expansion gives

$$\frac{3}{2}\left(1-\frac{x}{2}\right)^{-1} = \frac{3}{2}\left(1 + (-1)\left(-\frac{x}{2}\right) + \frac{(-1)(-1-1)}{2!}\left(\frac{-x}{2}\right)^2 + \ldots \right.$$
$$\left. \ldots \frac{(-1)(-1-1)(-1-2)}{3!}\left(\frac{-x}{2}\right)^3 + \ldots\right)$$

$$= \frac{3}{2}\left(1 + \frac{x}{2} + \frac{x^2}{4} + \frac{x^3}{8} + \ldots\right)$$

This expansion is valid for $-1 < -\frac{x}{2} < 1$ i.e. $-2 < x < 2$.

Using both expansions we have

$$\frac{1}{1+x} + \frac{3}{2-x} = (1 - x + x^2 - x^3 + \ldots) + \frac{3}{2}\left(1 + \frac{x}{2} + \frac{x^2}{4} + \frac{x^3}{8} + \ldots\right)$$

$$= \frac{5}{2} - \frac{x}{4} + \frac{11x^2}{8} - \frac{13x^3}{16} + \ldots$$

Therefore, the required series expansion is $\dfrac{5}{2} - \dfrac{x}{4} + \dfrac{11x^2}{8} - \dfrac{13x^3}{16}$.

This is valid for values of x that satisfy $-1 < x < 1$ and $-2 < x < 2$. Therefore, it is only valid for $-1 < x < 1$.

Key points

- The binomial expansion of $(1+x)^n$ is:
  - finite and valid for all x values if n is a positive integer
  - infinite and only valid for a range of x values if n is not a positive integer
- To find the binomial expansion of $(a+x)^n$, factorise to give $a^n\left(1+\frac{x}{a}\right)^n$ and then proceed by expanding $\left(1+\frac{x}{a}\right)^n$.
- To obtain the series expansion of algebraic fractions:
  - of the form $\dfrac{ax+b}{(cx+d)^n}$, write as $(ax+b)(cx+d)^{-n}$ and find the binomial expansion of $(cx+d)^{-n}$
  - which may be split into partial fractions, use partial fraction techniques and then expand each of the individual fractions

7

1 Trigonometric ratios

In the right-angled triangle,

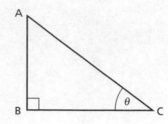

$$\sin\theta = \frac{AB}{AC}, \ \cos\theta = \frac{BC}{AC}, \ \tan\theta = \frac{AB}{BC}$$

1.1 STANDARD RATIOS

	30°	45°	60°
$\sin\theta$	$\frac{1}{2}$	$\frac{1}{\sqrt{2}}$	$\frac{\sqrt{3}}{2}$
$\cos\theta$	$\frac{\sqrt{3}}{2}$	$\frac{1}{\sqrt{2}}$	$\frac{1}{2}$
$\tan\theta$	$\frac{1}{\sqrt{3}}$	1	$\sqrt{3}$

These exact ratios should be used in questions that involve angles of 30°, 45° or 60° to ensure exact answers. Examination questions involving these angles and that use 'show' or 'prove' together with a stated result, usually require candidates to use exact ratios.

2 Graphs and properties of trigonometric functions

2.1 Y = SINθ

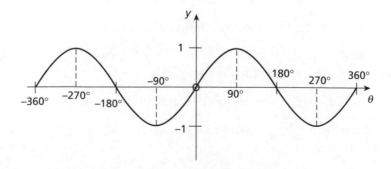

- The sine function is periodic, of period 360°.

- The sine function is an odd function.

- The maximum value of $\sin\theta$ is 1 and the minimum value is -1.

2.2 Y = cos θ

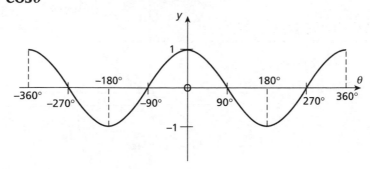

- The cosine function is periodic, of period 360°.

- The cosine function is an even function.

- The maximum value of cos θ is 1 and the minium value is −1.

2.3 Y = TAN θ

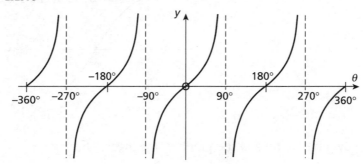

- The tangent function is periodic, of period 180°.

- The tangent function is an odd function.

- The tangent function is not defined when $\theta = \pm 90°, \pm 270°, \ldots$

3   *Inverse trigonometric functions*

We know that only one-to-one functions have inverses. It is clear that none of the functions sine, cosine or tangent are one-to-one in the domain of all real numbers. Restricting the domain of each will give one-to-one functions.

3.1 Y = SIN θ

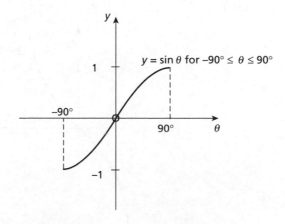

This is now one-to-one and the graph of the inverse function is

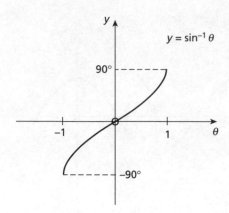

$y = \sin^{-1}\theta$

3.2 Y = cos θ

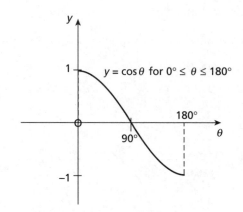

$y = \cos\theta$ for $0° \leq \theta \leq 180°$

This is now one-to-one and the graph of the inverse function is

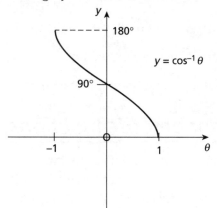

$y = \cos^{-1}\theta$

3.3 Y = TAN θ

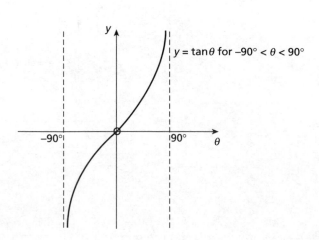

$y = \tan\theta$ for $-90° < \theta < 90°$

This is now one-to-one and the graph of the inverse function is

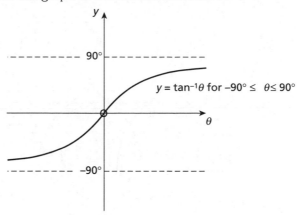

$y = \tan^{-1}\theta$ for $-90° \le \theta \le 90°$

Note: $\sin^{-1}\theta$ is the notation used for the inverse sine function, whereas $(\sin\theta)^{-1} = \dfrac{1}{\sin\theta}$ and is something different.

4 Further trigonometric functions: cosec θ, sec θ and cot θ

These trigonometric functions are defined as

$$\operatorname{cosec}\theta = \frac{1}{\sin\theta}, \ \sec\theta = \frac{1}{\cos\theta}, \ \cot\theta = \frac{1}{\tan\theta}$$

4.1 Y = COSEC θ

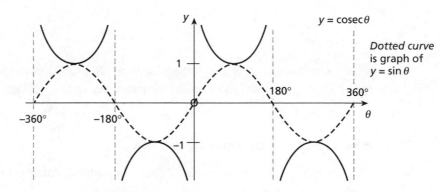

$y = \operatorname{cosec}\theta$

Dotted curve is graph of $y = \sin\theta$

4.2 Y = SEC θ

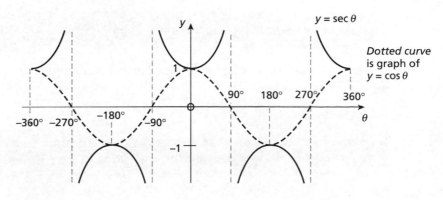

$y = \sec\theta$

Dotted curve is graph of $y = \cos\theta$

4.3 $y = \cot\theta$

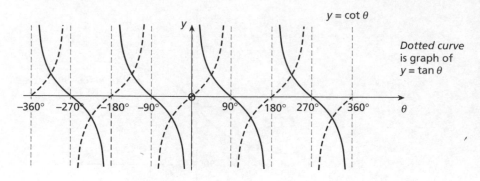

$y = \cot \theta$

Dotted curve is graph of $y = \tan \theta$

5 Radian measure

1 radian is defined as the angle subtended at the centre of a circle by an arc of length equal to the radius of the circle.

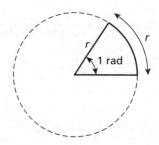

Since there are 360° at the centre of the circle and a circle of radius 1 has circumference 2π,

$$2\pi \text{ radians} = 360°$$
$$\therefore \qquad \pi \text{ radians} = 180°$$

Note: some examination questions request answers to be expressed in terms of radians. Some of the examples that follow are in terms of radians, while others are in terms of degrees.

5.1 ARC LENGTH AND AREA OF SECTOR

- The arc length, l, of the sector of a circle of radius r that subtends an angle of θ radians at the centre is given by

$$l = r\theta$$

> When θ is measured in degrees, the formula is given by $l = \dfrac{\theta}{360°} \times 2\pi r$.

- The area of a sector, A, of a circle of radius r that subtends an angle of θ radians at the centre is given by

$$A = \frac{1}{2}r^2\theta$$

> When θ is measured in degrees, the formula is given by $A = \dfrac{\theta}{360°} \times \pi r^2$.

6 Trigonometric identities

For any angle θ (i.e. not just acute angles), we have the following trigonometric identities:

- $\tan\theta = \dfrac{\sin\theta}{\cos\theta}$

- $\sin^2\theta + \cos^2\theta = 1$

- $1 + \tan^2\theta = \sec^2\theta$

- $1 + \cot^2\theta = \operatorname{cosec}^2\theta$

Example

Given that θ is acute and $\cos\theta = \dfrac{1}{\sqrt{5}}$, find the values of

(i) $\sin\theta$

(ii) $\tan\theta$

Solution

(i) If $\cos\theta = \dfrac{1}{\sqrt{5}}$, then $\cos^2\theta = \dfrac{1}{5}$. Using $\sin^2\theta + \cos^2\theta = 1$ gives

$$\sin^2\theta + \frac{1}{5} = 1$$

$$\therefore \qquad \sin^2\theta = 1 - \frac{1}{5} = \frac{4}{5}$$

$$\therefore \qquad \sin\theta = \frac{2}{\sqrt{5}} \text{ (a negative answer would correspond to non-acute value of } \theta)$$

(ii) Using $\tan\theta = \dfrac{\sin\theta}{\cos\theta}$ gives

$$\tan\theta = \frac{\left(\dfrac{2}{\sqrt{5}}\right)}{\left(\dfrac{1}{\sqrt{5}}\right)}$$

$$\therefore \quad \tan\theta = 2$$

7 Trigonometric equations

A trigonometric equation is always accompanied by a range for the angle, otherwise there would be an infinite number of solutions.

7.1 Solving equations of the form $\sin\theta = \kappa$, $\cos\theta = \kappa$, $\tan\theta = \kappa$

Example

Solve $\cos\theta = \dfrac{1}{5}$, where $0 \leq \theta \leq 360°$.

Solution

Sketching the graph of $y = \cos\theta$ for $0 \leq \theta \leq 360°$ shows the number of solutions.

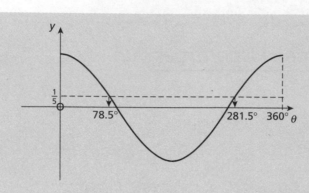

The calculator gives $\theta = 78.5°$, to one decimal place.

The other solution in the range is $\theta = 360° - 78.5° = 281.5°$.

The solutions are $\theta = 78.5°$ and $\theta = 281.5°$.

7.2 SOLVING EQUATIONS OF THE FORM $\operatorname{cosec}\theta = \kappa$, $\sec\theta = \kappa$, $\cot\theta = \kappa$

In these cases, transform to sine, cosine and tangent ratios and then solve.

Example

Solve $\cot\theta = 3$, where $0° \leq \theta \leq 360°$.

Solution

If $\cot\theta = 3$, then

$$\frac{1}{\tan\theta} = 3$$

$$\therefore \quad \tan\theta = \frac{1}{3}$$

In the range given there are two solutions, as illustrated below:

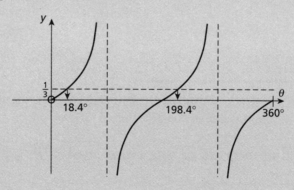

These are $\theta = 18.4°$ and $\theta = 180° + 18.4° = 198.4°$.

The solutions are $\theta = 18.4°$ and $\theta = 198.4°$.

7.3 USING MANIPULATION

Trigonometric equations may require some manipulation before they can be solved using the method illustrated above.

Example

Solve $3\sin^2\theta + \sin\theta = 0$, where $-180° \le \theta \le 180°$.

Solution

In this case, we notice that the equation is a quadratic in $\sin\theta$. Factorising and solving gives

$$\sin\theta\,(3\sin\theta + 1) = 0$$

$$\therefore \qquad \sin\theta = 0 \text{ or } 3\sin\theta + 1 = 0$$

$$\therefore \qquad \sin\theta = 0 \text{ or } \sin\theta = -\frac{1}{3}$$

When $\sin\theta = 0$, $\theta = 0°, \pm180°$, in the range given.

When $\sin\theta = -\frac{1}{3}$ we have two solutions in the range given.

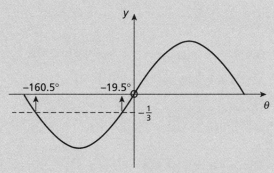

The calculator gives $\theta = -19.5°$, to one decimal place.

The other solution in the range is $\theta = -(180° - 19.5°) = -160.5°$.

The solutions are $\theta = 0°, \pm180°, -19.5°$ and $-160.5°$.

Using trigonometric identities

The manipulation may involve the use of a trigonometric identity.

Example

Solve $2\sin^2\theta + \cos\theta - 1 = 0$, where $0° \le \theta \le 2\pi$.

Solution

In this case, notice that the equation contains both sine and cosine ratios. The fact that it contains $\sin^2\theta$ suggests the use of the identity $\sin^2\theta + \cos^2\theta = 1$, thus expressing the equation in terms of the cosine function only.

From $\sin^2\theta + \cos^2\theta = 1$, we have $\sin^2\theta = 1 - \cos^2\theta$, substituting into $2\sin^2\theta + \cos\theta - 1 = 0$ gives

$$2(1 - \cos^2\theta) + \cos\theta - 1 = 0$$

$$\therefore \quad 2 - 2\cos^2\theta + \cos\theta - 1 = 0$$

$$\therefore \quad -2\cos^2\theta + \cos\theta + 1 = 0$$

$$\therefore \qquad 2\cos^2\theta - \cos\theta - 1 = 0$$

$$\therefore \qquad (2\cos\theta + 1)(\cos\theta - 1) = 0$$

$$\therefore \qquad \cos\theta = -\frac{1}{2} \text{ or } \cos\theta = 1$$

When $\cos\theta = -\frac{1}{2}$, there are two solutions in the given range.

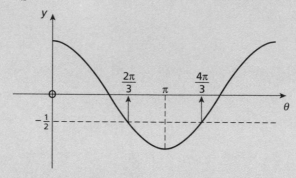

One value is $\theta = \frac{2\pi}{3}$.

The other solution in the range is $\theta = 2\pi - \frac{2\pi}{3} = \frac{4\pi}{3}$.

When $\cos\theta = 1$, $\theta = 0$ and 2π.

The solutions in radians are $\theta = 0, \frac{2\pi}{3}, \frac{4\pi}{3}$ and 2π.

Example

Solve $3 - \tan\theta = \sec^2\theta$, where $-180° \leq \theta \leq 180°$.

Solution

Using $\sec^2\theta = 1 + \tan^2\theta$ gives

$$3 - \tan\theta = 1 + \tan^2\theta$$

$$\therefore \qquad 1 + \tan^2\theta - 3 + \tan\theta = 0$$

$$\therefore \qquad \tan^2\theta + \tan\theta - 2 = 0$$

$$\therefore \qquad (\tan\theta - 1)(\tan\theta + 2) = 0$$

$$\therefore \qquad \tan\theta = 1 \text{ or } \tan\theta = -2$$

When $\tan\theta = 1$, there are two solutions in the given range:

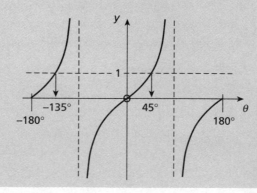

These are $\theta = 45°$ and $\theta = -(180° - 45°) = -135°$.

When $\tan\theta = -2$, there are two solutions in the given range.

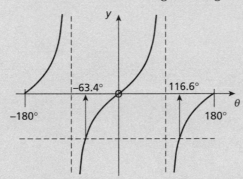

To one decimal place, these are $\theta = -63.4°$ and $\theta = 180° - 63.4° = 116.6°$.

The solutions are $\theta = 45°, -135°, -63.4°$ and $116.6°$.

7.4 TRIGONOMETRIC EQUATIONS INVOLVING MULTIPLE ANGLES

These involve angles of 2θ, 3θ, etc.

When solving trigonometric equations that involve multiple angles, it is important to change the range to match the multiple angle; otherwise possible solutions will be missed.

Example

Solve $\tan 2\theta = \frac{1}{2}$, where $0° \le \theta \le 360°$.

Solution

Changing the range gives $0° \le 2\theta \le 720°$.

When $\tan 2\theta = \frac{1}{2}$ we have four solutions in the range.

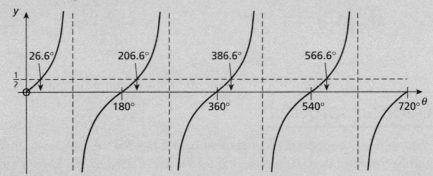

The calculator gives $2\theta = 26.6°$, to one decimal place.

The other solutions in the range are given by

$$2\theta = 180° + 26.6° = 206.6°$$

$$2\theta = 360° + 26.6° = 386.6°$$

$$2\theta = 540° + 26.6° = 566.6°$$

If $2\theta = 26.6°, 206.6°, 386.6°, 566.6°$ then $\theta = 13.3°, 103.3°, 193.3°, 283.3°$.

Note: a common error is to solve $\tan 2\theta = \frac{1}{2}$ giving the first solution as $\theta = 13.3°$ and then to calculate the other solutions as $\theta = 13.3° + 180°$, $\theta = 13.3° + 360°$ etc., which is clearly incorrect.

Example

Solve $\cos\left(3\theta + \frac{\pi}{6}\right) = \frac{1}{2}$, where $0° \leq \theta \leq \pi$.

Solution

Changing the range gives $\frac{\pi}{6} \leq 3\theta + \frac{\pi}{6} \leq \frac{19\pi}{6}$.

(Notice that $3(\pi) + \frac{\pi}{6} = \frac{19\pi}{6}$.)

When $\cos\left(3\theta + \frac{\pi}{6}\right) = \frac{1}{2}$, there are three solutions in the range.

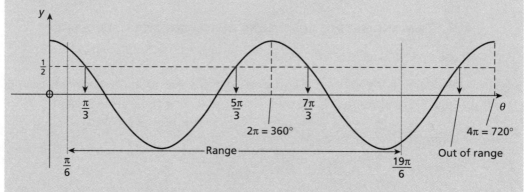

We know that $3\theta + \frac{\pi}{6} = \frac{\pi}{3}$.

The other solutions in the range are given by

$$3\theta + \frac{\pi}{6} = 2\pi - \frac{\pi}{3} = \frac{5\pi}{3}$$

$$3\theta + \frac{\pi}{6} = 2\pi + \frac{\pi}{3} = \frac{7\pi}{3}$$

If $3\theta + \frac{\pi}{6} = \frac{\pi}{3}, \frac{5\pi}{3}, \frac{7\pi}{3}$ then $\theta = \frac{\pi}{18}, \frac{\pi}{2}, \frac{13\pi}{18}$.

8 | *General solutions*

Trigonometric equations accompanied by a range for the unknown angle have a finite number of solutions. However, due to the periodicity of the trigonometric functions, general solutions to trigonometric equations can be derived.

Example

Write down the general solution, in radians, of the equation $\sin\theta = \frac{1}{2}$.

Solution

When $\sin\theta = \frac{1}{2}$, $\theta = 30° = \frac{\pi}{6}$ radians. From the graph below, we see that $\theta = 150° = \frac{5\pi}{6}$ radians also.

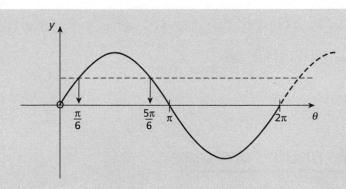

Since the sine function is of period 2π, we have

$$\theta = \frac{\pi}{6} + 2\pi \text{ and } \theta = \frac{5\pi}{6} + 2\pi$$

as solutions.

Generally, the solutions are

$$\theta = \frac{\pi}{6} + 2n\pi \text{ or } \theta = \frac{5\pi}{6} + 2n\pi$$

where n is an integer.

Example

Write down the general solution, in radians, of the equation $\tan\theta = \sqrt{3}$.

Solution

When $\tan\theta = \sqrt{3}$, $\theta = \frac{\pi}{3}$.

Since the tangent function is of period π, we have the general solution

$$\theta = \frac{\pi}{3} + n\pi$$

Key points

- Look for the range given in the question and ensure that this is the range that is used when finding the multiple solutions.

- Reduce trigonometric equations to one of the forms $\sin\theta = k$, $\cos\theta = k$ or $\tan\theta = k$ and solve.

- When solving $\sin n\theta = k$, $\cos n\theta = k$ or $\tan n\theta = k$, change the range given for θ to a range for $n\theta$ and solve.

- Check to see whether the question requires a general solution, in which case you should not give a list of different numerical solutions.

9   Compound angles

For any angles A and B, we have:

- $\sin(A \pm B) = \sin A \cos B \pm \cos A \sin B$

- $\cos(A \pm B) = \cos A \cos B \mp \sin A \sin B$

- $\tan(A \pm B) = \dfrac{\tan A \pm \tan B}{1 \mp \tan A \tan B}$

Note: a common error is to write $\sin(15° + 30°) = \sin 15° + \sin 30°$. Calculating the value of both sides shows this is not the case.

10 *Double angle formulae*

For any angle A, we have:

- $\sin 2A = 2 \sin A \cos A$

- $\cos 2A = \cos^2 A - \sin^2 A$

$$= 2\cos^2 A - 1$$

$$= 1 - 2\sin^2 A$$

- $\tan 2A = \dfrac{2\tan A}{1 - \tan^2 A}$

Each of these is easy to derive from the compound angle formulae. For example,

$$\tan(A + B) = \frac{\tan A + \tan B}{1 - \tan A \tan A}$$

Let $B = A$, then

$$\tan(A + A) = \tan 2A = \frac{\tan A + \tan A}{1 - \tan A \tan A}$$

$$= \frac{2\tan A}{1 - \tan^2 A}, \text{ as required}$$

Example

Given that A and B are acute angles, that $\sin A = \dfrac{12}{13}$ and that $\cos B = \dfrac{4}{5}$, find the value of $\sin(A - B)$.

Solution

When $\sin A = \dfrac{12}{13}$ and A is acute, $\cos A = \dfrac{5}{13}$, as can be seen from the right-angled triangle.

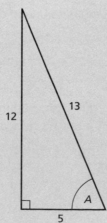

13
12
5
A

When $\cos B = \frac{4}{5}$ and B is acute, $\sin B = \frac{3}{5}$, as can be seen from the right-angled triangle.

Now,

$$\sin(A - B) = \sin A \cos B - \cos A \sin B$$
$$= \frac{12}{13} \cdot \frac{4}{5} - \frac{5}{13} \cdot \frac{3}{5}$$
$$= \frac{48}{65} - \frac{3}{13}$$
$$= \frac{33}{65}$$

10.1 FURTHER TRIGONOMETRIC EQUATIONS

Example

Solve $\cos\theta \cos 30° - \sin\theta \sin 30° = \frac{1}{3}$, where $0° \le \theta \le 180°$.

Solution

It is important to observe that the LHS is the same as $\cos(\theta + 30°)$. Therefore, the equation can be written as

$$\cos(\theta + 30°) = \frac{1}{3}$$

Changing the range to match $\theta + 30°$, gives $30° \le \theta + 30° \le 210°$:

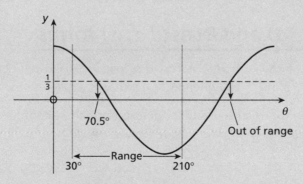

Solving gives $\theta + 30° = 70.5°$, to one decimal place. Therefore, $\theta = 40.5°$.

11 Solving trigonometric equations

Trigonometric equations may involve double angles, which are not in the standard form $\sin 2\theta = k$, $\cos 2\theta = k$, $\tan 2\theta = k$, where k is a constant. The following example illustrates such a case.

Example

Solve $\cos 2\theta + \sin\theta - 1 = 0$, where $0° \le \theta \le 360°$.

Solution

In this case, there are three possible identities for $\cos 2\theta$. Clearly, using $\cos 2\theta = 1 - 2\sin^2\theta$ will result in the equation being expressed in terms of the sine function only. Substituting gives

$$1 - 2\sin^2\theta + \sin\theta - 1 = 0$$

$$\therefore \qquad 2\sin^2\theta - \sin\theta = 0$$

$$\therefore \qquad \sin\theta\,(2\sin\theta - 1) = 0$$

$$\therefore \qquad \sin\theta = 0 \text{ or } \sin\theta = \frac{1}{2}$$

When $\sin\theta = 0$, $\theta = 0°, 180°, 360°$ in the given range.

When $\sin\theta = \frac{1}{2}$, there are two solutions in the given range.

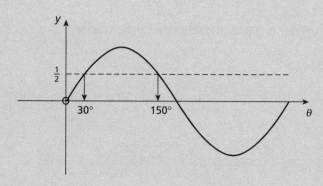

Solving gives $\theta = 30°$ and $\theta = 180° - 30° = 150°$.

The solutions are $\theta = 0°, 180°, 360°, 30°$ and $150°$.

12 $R\sin(\theta \pm \alpha)$ and $R\cos(\theta \pm \alpha)$ forms

- Functions of the form $f(\theta) = a\cos\theta + b\sin\theta$ can be expressed in the form $R\cos(\theta \pm \alpha)$ or $R\sin(\theta \pm \alpha)$, where $R > 0$ and α is acute.

- This alternative form is useful for determining the maximum and minimum values of the function $f(\theta)$ and for solving equations $f(\theta) = 0$.

Example

(i) Express $2\cos\theta - 3\sin\theta$ in the form $R\cos(\theta + \alpha)$.

(ii) Determine the maximum and minimum values of the function
$f(\theta) = 2\cos\theta - 3\sin\theta$

(iii) Solve the equation $2\cos\theta - 3\sin\theta = 1$, for $0° \leq \theta \leq 360°$

Solution

(i) Let $2\cos\theta - 3\sin\theta = R\cos(\theta + \alpha)$

$$= R\cos\theta\cos\alpha - R\sin\theta\sin\alpha$$

Equating coefficients of $\cos\theta$ and $\sin\theta$ gives

$R\cos\alpha = 2$ (1)   and $R\sin\alpha = 3$ (2)

Dividing (2) by (1) gives

$$\frac{R\sin\alpha}{R\cos\alpha} = \frac{3}{2}$$

$\therefore$ $\tan\alpha = \dfrac{3}{2}$

$\therefore$ $\alpha = 56.3°$

Squaring both (1) and (2) and adding gives

$R^2\cos^2\alpha + R^2\sin^2\alpha = 2^2 + 3^2$

$\therefore$ $R^2(\cos^2\alpha + \sin^2\alpha) = 13$

$\therefore$ $R^2 = 13$, since $\cos^2\alpha + \sin^2\alpha = 1$

$\therefore$ $R = \sqrt{13}$

Therefore, $2\cos\theta - 3\sin\theta = \sqrt{13}\cos(\theta + 56.3°)$

(ii) Now, $f(\theta) = \sqrt{13}\cos(\theta + 56.3°)$.

The function f attains its maximum value when the cosine function attains its maximum value. The cosine function has a maximum value of 1. Therefore, the maximum value of f is $\sqrt{13}$.

Similarly, the function f attains its minimum value when the cosine function attains its minimum value of -1. Therefore, the minimum value of f is $-\sqrt{13}$.

(iii) The equation $2\cos\theta - 3\sin\theta = 1$ can be written as

$\sqrt{13}\cos(\theta + 56.3°) = 1$

$\therefore$ $\cos(\theta + 56.3°) = \dfrac{1}{\sqrt{13}}$

Changing the range, gives $56.3° \leq \theta + 56.3° \leq 416.3°$.

Solving, gives

$\theta + 56.3° = 73.9°$

$\therefore$ $\theta = 17.6°$

The other solution in the range is

$\theta + 56.3° = 360° - 73.9°$

$\therefore$ $\theta = 229.8°$

The solutions are $\theta = 17.6°$ and $\theta = 229.8°$.

Important note

In the above example, the question gives the required form, namely $R\cos(\theta + \alpha)$. In some cases, the question may not specify. Some examples are shown below:

- given the form $a\cos\theta + b\sin\theta$ in the question, then use $R\cos(\theta - \alpha)$

- given the form $a\sin\theta - b\cos\theta$ in the question, then use $R\sin(\theta - \alpha)$

13 *Small angle approximations*

For small angles θ, measured in radians, the following approximations hold:

(i) $\sin\theta \approx \theta$

(ii) $\cos\theta \approx 1 - \frac{1}{2}\theta^2$

(iii) $\tan\theta \approx \theta$

These approximations only hold if θ is small and measured in radians.

Approximations (i) and (iii) can be seen by considering the graphs of $y = \sin\theta$, $y = \tan\theta$ and $y = \theta$.

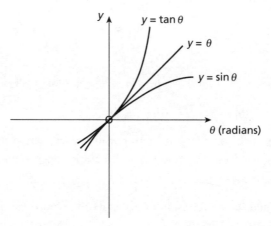

Similarly, approximation (ii) can be seen by considering the graphs of $y = \cos\theta$ and $y = 1 - \frac{1}{2}\theta^2$.

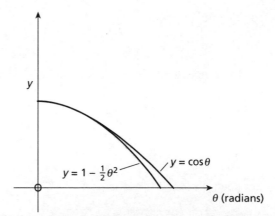

Example

Find an approximation for $\dfrac{1 - \cos\theta}{\theta^2}$ when θ is small.

Solution

Using $\cos\theta \approx 1 - \frac{1}{2}\theta^2$, gives

$$\frac{1 - \cos\theta}{\theta^2} \approx \frac{1 - \left(1 - \frac{1}{2}\theta^2\right)}{\theta^2}$$

$$\therefore \quad \frac{1 - \cos\theta}{\theta^2} \approx \frac{\left(\frac{1}{2}\theta^2\right)}{\theta^2}$$

$$= \frac{1}{2}$$

Therefore, when θ is small, $\dfrac{1 - \cos\theta}{\theta^2} \approx \dfrac{1}{2}$

Example

In the triangle ABC, AB = 1 unit, AC = 4 units and the angle BAC is θ radians.

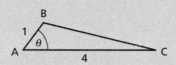

Given that θ is small, show that BC $\approx (9 + 4\theta^2)^{\frac{1}{2}}$.

Solution

Using the cosine rule,

$$BC^2 = AB^2 + AC^2 - 2(AB)(AC)\cos\theta$$

$$BC^2 = 1 + 16 - 8\cos\theta$$

$$BC^2 = 17 - 8\cos\theta$$

Using $\cos\theta \approx 1 - \dfrac{1}{2}\theta^2$ gives

$$BC^2 = 17 - 8\left(1 - \frac{1}{2}\theta^2\right)$$

$$\therefore \quad BC^2 = 9 + 4\theta^2$$

$$\therefore \quad BC = (9 + 4\theta^2)^{\frac{1}{2}}, \text{ as required}$$

TOPIC 8 Calculus I: differentiation

1 Gradient of a curve

The gradient of a curve at a point P is defined as the gradient of the tangent line to the curve at the point P.

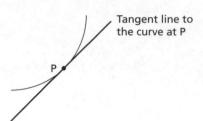

Tangent line to the curve at P

P

Note: the gradient of a curve is different at different points.

2 Differentiation from first principles

Drawing tangent lines by eye in order to find the gradient of a curve at a particular point is inaccurate. Differentiation is a precise method for finding the gradient.

The first derivative of a function $f(x)$ is defined as

$$f'(x) = \lim_{h \to 0} \left\{ \frac{f(x + h) - f(x)}{h} \right\}$$

where h is some small increase in x.

Note: if the function is expressed in the form $y =$ 'some expression in x', then the first derivative is defined as

$$\frac{dy}{dx} = \lim_{\delta x \to 0} \frac{\delta y}{\delta x}$$

where δx is a small increase in x and δy is a small increase in y.

The first derivative is sometimes referred to as the gradient function, because it is this that gives the exact gradient of the curve at any point P.

Example

Given that $f(x) = x^2$, find the first derivative, $f'(x)$.

Solution

Using the definition $f'(x) = \lim_{h \to 0} \left\{ \frac{f(x + h) - f(x)}{h} \right\}$ gives

$$f'(x) = \lim_{h \to 0} \left\{ \frac{(x + h)^2 - x^2}{h} \right\}$$

$$= \lim_{h \to 0} \left\{ \frac{x^2 + 2xh + h^2 - x^2}{h} \right\}$$

$$= \lim_{h \to 0} \left(\frac{2xh + h^2}{h} \right)$$

$$\therefore \quad f'(x) = \lim_{h \to 0} (2x + h)$$

Now, as h tends to zero, $2x + h \to 2x$.

Therefore,

$$f'(x) = 2x$$

Note: this process is called 'differentiation from first principles'.

This now enables the calculation of the gradient of the curve defined by $f(x) = x^2$ at any point. For example:

- the gradient at the point where $x = 3$ is given by $f'(3) = 2 \times 3 = 6$
- the gradient at the point $(-1, 1)$ is given by $f'(-1) = 2(-1) = -2$

3   *Differentiation of x^n and Ax^n*

- If $y = x^n$, then it can be shown that the first derivative, written as $\dfrac{dy}{dx}$, is nx^{n-1}.
- If $y = Ax^n$, then $\dfrac{dy}{dx} = Anx^{n-1}$.

This is a very powerful result and one that enables the first derivative to be found without having to go through the long process of 'differentiation from first principles' on every occasion.

It is useful to note the following two results, where k is a constant:

- if $y = k$, then $\dfrac{dy}{dx} = 0$
- if $y = kx$, then $\dfrac{dy}{dx} = k$

Example

Find the first derivative of each of the following functions:

(i) $y = 3x^2$

(ii) $y = \dfrac{1}{x}$

(iii) $y = \sqrt{x}$

The question does not ask for 'first principles', so the standard result can be used.

Solution

(i)   If $y = 3x^2$, then $\dfrac{dy}{dx} = 6x$

In (ii) and (iii) it is necessary to write y in the form x^n in order to use the standard result.

(ii)   If $y = \dfrac{1}{x} = x^{-1}$, then $\dfrac{dy}{dx} = (-1)\,x^{-2} = -\dfrac{1}{x^2}$

(iii) If $y = \sqrt{x} = x^{\frac{1}{2}}$, then $\dfrac{dy}{dx} = \dfrac{1}{2}x^{\frac{1}{2}-1} = \dfrac{1}{2}x^{-\frac{1}{2}} = \dfrac{1}{2} \cdot \dfrac{1}{x^{\frac{1}{2}}} = \dfrac{1}{2\sqrt{x}}$

When y comprises the sum or difference of a number of functions, the first derivative is found by differentiating each function in turn. In other words,

$$\dfrac{d}{dx}\{f(x) \pm g(x)\} = \dfrac{d}{dx}(f(x)) \pm \dfrac{d}{dx}(g(x))$$

TOPIC 8 Calculus I: differentiation

Example

Find the first derivative of each of the following functions:

(i) $y = x^3 + 5x$

(ii) $y = 2 + \dfrac{1}{\sqrt{x}}$

Solution

(i) If $y = x^3 + 5x$ then $\dfrac{dy}{dx} = 3x^2 + 5$

(ii) If $y = 2 + \dfrac{1}{\sqrt{x}} = 2 + x^{-\frac{1}{2}}$ then $\dfrac{dy}{dx} = 0 + (-\frac{1}{2})\,x^{-\frac{3}{2}} = -\frac{1}{2}\cdot\dfrac{1}{x^{\frac{3}{2}}} = -\dfrac{1}{2\sqrt{x^3}}$

In some cases, functions do not appear in the standard form and some algebraic manipulation is necessary. The following example illustrates this.

Example

Find $\dfrac{dy}{dx}$ for each of the following:

(i) $y = (x + 2)(x - 5)$

(ii) $y = \dfrac{2x^3 + x}{x^2}$

Solution

(i) Expanding the brackets and simplifying gives:

$$y = x^2 - 3x - 10$$

$$\therefore \quad \dfrac{dy}{dx} = 2x - 3$$

(ii) This can be expressed in the form $y = \dfrac{2x^3}{x^2} + \dfrac{x}{x^2} = 2x + \dfrac{1}{x} = 2x + x^{-1}$

Therefore, $\dfrac{dy}{dx} = 2 - x^{-2} = 2 - \dfrac{1}{x^2}$

4 Differentiation of e^{kx} and $\ln x$

- If $y = e^x$, then it can be shown that $\dfrac{dy}{dx} = e^x$.

- If $y = e^{kx}$, then it can be shown that $\dfrac{dy}{dx} = ke^{kx}$.

- If $y = \ln x$, then it can be shown that $\dfrac{dy}{dx} = \dfrac{1}{x}$.

Example

Find $\dfrac{dy}{dx}$ for each of the following:

(i) $y = e^{5x}$

(ii) $y = (1 + e^x)^2$

(iii) $y = \ln x + x$

(iv) $y = \ln \sqrt{x}$

Solution

(i) If $y = e^{5x}$ then $\dfrac{dy}{dx} = 5e^{5x}$.

(ii) Expanding the brackets gives

$$y = (1 + e^x)^2$$

$$= (1 + e^x)(1 + e^x)$$

$$= 1 + 2e^x + e^{2x}$$

Now, differentiating term by term gives

$$\frac{dy}{dx} = 2e^x + 2e^{2x}$$

(iii) If $y = \ln x + x$ then $\dfrac{dy}{dx} = \dfrac{1}{x} + 1$.

(iv) Using rules of logarithms gives

$$y = \ln \sqrt{x}$$

$$= \ln x^{\frac{1}{2}}$$

$$= \frac{1}{2}\ln x$$

Therefore,

$$\frac{dy}{dx} = \frac{1}{2} \cdot \frac{1}{x}$$

$$= \frac{1}{2x}$$

5 *Differentiation of trigonometric functions*

- If $y = \sin ax$, then $\dfrac{dy}{dx} = a\cos ax$, where x is measured in radians.

- If $y = \cos ax$, then $\dfrac{dy}{dx} = -a\sin ax$, where x is measured in radians.

- If $y = \tan ax$, then $\dfrac{dy}{dx} = a\sec^2 ax$, where x is measured in radians.

Example

Find $\dfrac{dy}{dx}$ for each of the following:

(i) $y = 3\sin x + 2\cos x$

(ii) $y = \dfrac{4\sin x}{\cos x}$

Solution

(i) If $y = 3\sin x + 2\cos x$, then $\dfrac{dy}{dx} = 3\cos x - 2\sin x$.

(ii) Using $\dfrac{\sin x}{\cos x} = \tan x$ gives

$$y = \frac{4\sin x}{\cos x} = 4\tan x$$

Therefore,

$$\frac{dy}{dx} = 4\sec^2 x$$

Key points

- $f'(x) = \lim\limits_{h \to 0} \left\{ \dfrac{f(x + h) - f(x)}{h} \right\}$ is the first derivative.

  (Only use this if the question asks for the first derivative from first principles.)

- If $y = Ax^n$ then $\dfrac{dy}{dx} = Anx^{n-1}$.

  (An alternative notation is $f(x) = Ax^n$ then $f'(x) = Anx^{n-1}$.)

- If $y = e^{kx}$, then $\dfrac{dy}{dx} = ke^{kx}$, k constant.

- If $y = \ln x$, then $\dfrac{dy}{dx} = \dfrac{1}{x}$.

- If $y = \sin ax$, then $\dfrac{dy}{dx} = a\cos ax$.

- If $y = \cos ax$, then $\dfrac{dy}{dx} = -a\sin ax$.

- If $y = \tan ax$, then $\dfrac{dy}{dx} = a\sec^2 ax$.

6 | *Tangents and normals*

- The normal to a curve at a point P is the straight line through P which is perpendicular to the tangent at P.

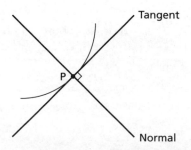

Example

Find the equation of the tangent to the curve $y = \dfrac{1}{x^2}$ at the point P $\left(2, \dfrac{1}{4}\right)$

Solution

The gradient of the tangent at P is given by $\frac{dy}{dx}$ evaluated at P.

If $y = \frac{1}{x^2} = x^{-2}$, then $\frac{dy}{dx} = -2x^{-3} = -\frac{2}{x^3}$

At P $\left(2, \frac{1}{4}\right)$: $\frac{dy}{dx} = -\frac{2}{(2)^3} = -\frac{1}{4}$

The tangent at P is given by $y = mx + c$, i.e. $y = -\frac{1}{4}x + c$. The tangent line passes through P $\left(2, \frac{1}{4}\right)$. Therefore,

$$\frac{1}{4} = -\frac{1}{4}(2) + c$$

$$\therefore \quad c = \frac{3}{4}$$

The equation of the tangent is $y = -\frac{1}{4}x + \frac{3}{4}$ or $4y = -x + 3$, i.e. $4y + x - 3 = 0$

Example

Find the equation of the normal to the curve $y = \cos x$ at the point P $\left(\frac{\pi}{2}, 0\right)$

Solution

If $y = \cos x$ then $\frac{dy}{dx} = -\sin x$.

At P $\left(\frac{\pi}{2}, 0\right)$: $\frac{dy}{dx} = -\sin\left(\frac{\pi}{2}\right) = -1$

The gradient of the tangent line at P is -1. Therefore, the gradient of the normal at P is $\frac{-1}{(-1)} = 1$. (The tangent and normal are perpendicular lines.)

The normal at P is given by $y = mx + c$, i.e. $y = 1x + c$. The normal line passes through P $\left(\frac{\pi}{2}, 0\right)$. Therefore,

$$0 = \left(\frac{\pi}{2}\right) + c$$

$$\therefore \quad c = -\frac{\pi}{2}$$

The equation of the normal is $y = x - \frac{\pi}{2}$.

7   *Increasing and decreasing functions*

- When $\frac{dy}{dx}$ is positive, the graph has a positive gradient. As the value of x increases, so does the value of y. In this case, y is an **increasing function.**

- When $\frac{dy}{dx}$ is negative, the graph has a negative gradient. As the value of x increases, the value of y decreases. In this case, y is a **decreasing function.**

Some functions are increasing/decreasing for all values of x, while others are increasing for some values of x and decreasing for others. The two graphs below illustrate these cases.

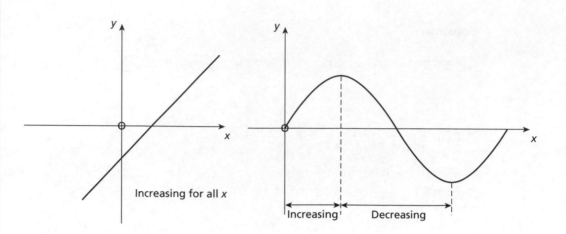

Increasing for all x

Increasing   Decreasing

Example

Determine the intervals of increase and of decrease for each of the following functions:

(i) $y = x - x^2$

(ii) $y = \sin x - x$

Solution

(i) If $y = x - x^2$ then $\dfrac{dy}{dx} = 1 - 2x$.

We see that $\dfrac{dy}{dx} > 0$ for $x < \dfrac{1}{2}$ and $\dfrac{dy}{dx} < 0$ for $x > \dfrac{1}{2}$.

The function is increasing for $x < \dfrac{1}{2}$ and decreasing for $x > \dfrac{1}{2}$. A sketch graph shows this:

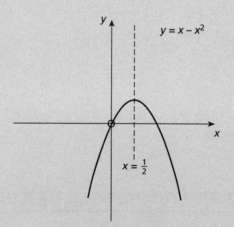

$y = x - x^2$

$x = \dfrac{1}{2}$

(ii) If $y = \sin x - x$ then $\dfrac{dy}{dx} = \cos x - 1$.

Now, $\cos x - 1 \leq 0$ for all values of x.

Therefore, $y = \sin x - x$ is a decreasing function for all values of x. A sketch graph shows this:

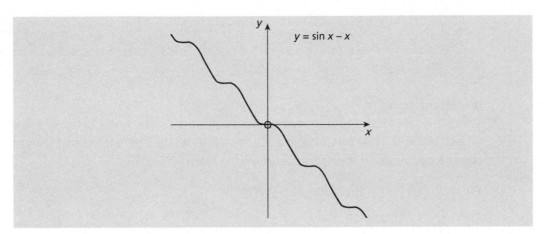

Key points

- Evaluating $\frac{dy}{dx}$ at a point gives the gradient of the curve (and the tangent line to the curve) at that point.

- The normal line is perpendicular to the tangent line. If the gradient of the tangent line is m, the gradient of the normal line is $-\frac{1}{m}$.

- If $\frac{dy}{dx}$ is positive for a particular x-interval, we say that the corresponding function is increasing on the interval.

- If $\frac{dy}{dx}$ is negative for a particular x-interval, we say that the corresponding function is decreasing on the interval.

8 Differentiation of a function of a function (chain rule)

Some functions are composite functions and as such can be differentiated using the **chain rule**. An example of a composite function is $y = \sin x^2$; this is the composite of the two functions $\sin x$ and x^2. In other words, if $f(x) = \sin x$ and $g(x) = x^2$, then $y = \sin x^2 = f(g(x)) = f \circ g$.

8.1 The chain rule

- If y is a function of u and u is a function of x, then

$$\frac{dy}{dx} = \frac{dy}{du} \cdot \frac{du}{dx}$$

Example
By making a suitable substitution, find $\frac{dy}{dx}$ when $y = (x^2 + 1)^3$.

Solution
Let $u = x^2 + 1$, then $y = u^3$. Differentiating each of these functions gives $\frac{du}{dx} = 2x$ and $\frac{dy}{du} = 3u^2$. Using the chain rule gives

$$\frac{dy}{dx} = \frac{dy}{du} \cdot \frac{du}{dx} = 3u^2 \times 2x = 3(x^2 + 1)^2 \times 2x$$

$$\therefore \quad \frac{dy}{dx} = 6x(x^2 + 1)^2$$

Note: in this particular example expansion of the bracket $(x^2 + 1)^3$ would give y as a polynomial and each term could be differentiated in turn. However, this is long and complicated and is not always possible.

Important point

There is no need to show the substitution explicitly, as illustrated in the example above, unless the question specifically asks for such detail. The process of differentiating composite functions is much simpler and is illustrated below.

Write the composite function as $y = f(g(x))$.

Then $\dfrac{dy}{dx} = f'(g(x))g'(x)$.

This means that in the previous example, $y = (x^2 + 1)^3$

$$\frac{dy}{dx} = 3(x^2 + 1)^2 (x^2 + 1)', \text{ where } (x^2 + 1)' = \frac{d}{dx}(x^2 + 1)$$

$$\therefore \quad \frac{dy}{dx} = 3 (x^2 + 1)^2 \, 2x = 6x(x^2 + 1)^2$$

Example

Find $\dfrac{dy}{dx}$ for each of the following:

(i) $y = \sqrt{x^2 + 1}$

(ii) $y = \sin 5x$

(iii) $y = \ln(x^2 - 2)$

(iv) $y = \cos^2 x$

(v) $y = \dfrac{1}{3x - 2}$

Solution

(i) If $y = \sqrt{x^2 + 1} = (x^2 + 1)^{\frac{1}{2}}$, then

$$\frac{dy}{dx} = \frac{1}{2}(x^2 + 1)^{-\frac{1}{2}} \times (x^2 + 1)'$$

$$= \frac{1}{2} \cdot \frac{1}{\sqrt{x^2 + 1}} \times 2x$$

$$\therefore \quad \frac{dy}{dx} = \frac{x}{\sqrt{x^2 + 1}}$$

(ii) If $y = \sin 5x = \sin(5x)$, then

$$\frac{dy}{dx} = \cos(5x) \times (5x)'$$

$$= 5\cos 5x$$

(iii) If $y = \ln(x^2 - 2)$ then

$$\frac{dy}{dx} = \frac{1}{x^2 - 2} \times (x^2 - 2)'$$

$$= \frac{2x}{x^2 - 2}$$

(iv) If $y = \cos^2 x = (\cos x)^2$, then

$$\frac{dy}{dx} = 2(\cos x) \times (\cos x)'$$

$$= 2\cos x \times (-\sin x)$$

$$= -2\sin x \cos x$$

$$\therefore \quad \frac{dy}{dx} = -\sin 2x, \text{ using the trigonometric identity } \sin 2x \equiv 2\sin x \cos x$$

(v) If $y = \dfrac{1}{3x - 2} = (3x - 2)^{-1}$, then

$$\frac{dy}{dx} = -(3x - 2)^{-2} \times (3x - 2)'$$

$$= -3(3x - 2)^{-2}$$

$$\therefore \quad \frac{dy}{dx} = -\frac{3}{(3x - 2)^2}$$

9 Further trigonometric results

9.1 THE FUNCTIONS SECANT, COSECANT AND COTANGENT

- If $y = \sec x$, then $\dfrac{dy}{dx} = \tan x \sec x$.

- If $y = \operatorname{cosec} x$, then $\dfrac{dy}{dx} = -\cot x \operatorname{cosec} x$.

- If $y = \cot x$, then $\dfrac{dy}{dx} = -\operatorname{cosec}^2 x$.

Each of these can be derived using the chain rule, together with the derivatives of the three standard trigonometric functions. Examination questions may ask for such derivations.

- If $y = \sec x = \dfrac{1}{\cos x} = (\cos x)^{-1}$, then

$$\frac{dy}{dx} = -1(\cos x)^{-2} \times (-\sin x)$$

$$= \frac{\sin x}{\cos^2 x}$$

$$= \frac{\sin x}{\cos x} \cdot \frac{1}{\cos x}$$

$$\therefore \quad \frac{dy}{dx} = \tan x \sec x, \text{ as required}$$

- If $y = \operatorname{cosec} x = \dfrac{1}{\sin x} = (\sin x)^{-1}$, then

$$\frac{dy}{dx} = -1(\sin x)^{-2} \times (\cos x)$$

$$= -\frac{\cos x}{\sin^2 x}$$

$$= -\frac{\cos x}{\sin x} \cdot \frac{1}{\sin x}$$

$$\therefore \quad \frac{dy}{dx} = -\cot x \operatorname{cosec} x, \text{ as required}$$

- If $y = \cot x = \dfrac{1}{\tan x} = (\tan x)^{-1}$, then

$$\frac{dy}{dx} = -1(\tan x)^{-2} \times (\sec^2 x)$$

$$= -\frac{\sec^2 x}{\tan^2 x}$$

$$= -\frac{1}{\cos^2 x} \times \frac{\cos^2 x}{\sin^2 x} = -\frac{1}{\sin^2 x}$$

$$\therefore \quad \frac{dy}{dx} = -\cosec^2 x, \text{ as required}$$

Example

Find $\dfrac{dy}{dx}$ for each of the following:

(i) $y = \sec 3x$

(ii) $y = \cot x^2$

(iii) $y = 4\cosec 2x$

Solution

(i) If $y = \sec 3x$, then using the chain rule,

$$\frac{dy}{dx} = \tan 3x \sec 3x \times (3x)'$$

$$= 3\tan 3x \sec 3x$$

(ii) If $y = \cot x^2$, then using the chain rule,

$$\frac{dy}{dx} = -\cosec^2(x^2) \times (x^2)'$$

$$= -2x\cosec^2(x^2)$$

(iii) If $y = 4\cosec 2x$, then using the chain rule,

$$\frac{dy}{dx} = 4(-\cot 2x \cosec 2x) \times (2x)'$$

$$= -8\cot 2x \cosec 2x$$

9.2 THE INVERSE TRIGONOMETRIC FUNCTIONS

- If $y = \sin^{-1} x$, then $\dfrac{dy}{dx} = \dfrac{1}{\sqrt{1-x^2}}$.

- If $y = \cos^{-1} x$, then $\dfrac{dy}{dx} = \dfrac{-1}{\sqrt{1-x^2}}$.

- If $y = \tan^{-1} x$, then $\dfrac{dy}{dx} = \dfrac{1}{1+x^2}$.

All three derivatives can be derived in similar ways. The derivation of the first result is as follows.

If $y = \sin^{-1} x$, then write this as $x = \sin y$ and differentiate with respect to y, giving

$$\frac{dx}{dy} = \cos y$$

Since $\dfrac{dy}{dx} = \dfrac{1}{\left(\dfrac{dx}{dy}\right)}$, we have

$$\frac{dy}{dx} = \frac{1}{\cos y}$$

Since $\sin^2 y + \cos^2 y = 1$, we have $\cos y = \sqrt{1 - \sin^2 y}$.

Substituting gives

$$\frac{dy}{dx} = \frac{1}{\sqrt{1 - \sin^2 y}}$$

$$= \frac{1}{\sqrt{1 - x2}}, \text{ as required.}$$

Example

Given that $y = \cos^{-1} x^2$, find $\dfrac{dy}{dx}$ when $x = \dfrac{1}{2}$.

Solution

If $y = \cos^{-1} x^2$, using the result for the first derivative of inverse cosine together with the chain rule gives

$$\frac{dy}{dx} = \frac{-1}{\sqrt{1 - (x^2)^2}} \times 2x$$

$$= \frac{-2x}{\sqrt{1 - x^4}}$$

When $x = \dfrac{1}{2}$, we have

$$\frac{dy}{dx} = \frac{-2\left(\frac{1}{2}\right)}{\sqrt{1 - \left(\frac{1}{2}\right)^4}}$$

$$= \frac{-1}{\sqrt{\frac{15}{16}}}$$

$$\therefore \quad \frac{dy}{dx} = \frac{-4}{\sqrt{15}}$$

10 *Differentiation of products and quotients*

The product rule and quotient rule are used when the function y can be expressed as a product or quotient of two functions. For example, $y = x^2 \sin x$ or $y = \frac{\ln x}{x^2}$.

10.1 THE PRODUCT RULE

If $y = u \cdot v$, where u and v are functions of x, then

$$\frac{dy}{dx} = u\frac{dv}{dx} + v\frac{du}{dx}$$

10.2 THE QUOTIENT RULE

If $y = \dfrac{u}{v}$, where u and v are functions of x, then

$$\frac{dy}{dx} = \frac{v\dfrac{du}{dx} - u\dfrac{dv}{dx}}{v^2}$$

Example

Find $\dfrac{dy}{dx}$ when $y = x^2 \sin x$.

Solution

If $y = x^2 \sin x$, then using the product rule gives

$$\frac{dy}{dx} = x^2 (\sin x)' + \sin x (x^2)'$$

$$= x^2 \cos x + 2x \sin x$$

Factorising gives

$$\frac{dy}{dx} = x(x \cos x + 2 \sin x)$$

Example

Find $\dfrac{dy}{dx}$ when $y = \dfrac{\ln x}{x^2}$.

Solution

If $y = \dfrac{\ln x}{x^2}$, then using the quotient rule gives

$$\frac{dy}{dx} = \frac{x^2 (\ln x)' - \ln x (x^2)'}{(x^2)^2}$$

$$= \frac{x^2 \times \dfrac{1}{x} - 2x \ln x}{x^4} = \frac{x - 2x \ln x}{x^4}$$

Factorising the numerator and simplifying gives

$$\frac{dy}{dx} = \frac{x(1 - 2\ln x)}{x^4} = \frac{1 - 2\ln x}{x^3}$$

10.3 PRODUCT, QUOTIENT AND CHAIN RULES

In some cases, it is necessary to use the product or quotient rule, and one of the functions u or v is composite, thus requiring use of the chain rule. The following example illustrates such a case.

Example

Find $\dfrac{dy}{dx}$ when $y = x^2 \sqrt{x^3 + 1}$.

Solution

If $y = x^2 \sqrt{x^3 + 1} = x^2 (x^3 + 1)^{\frac{1}{2}}$, then using the product rule gives

$$\frac{dy}{dx} = x^2 \left[(x^3 + 1)^{\frac{1}{2}} \right]' + (x^3 + 1)^{\frac{1}{2}} (x^2)'$$

$$= x^2 \left\{ \frac{1}{2} (x^3 + 1)^{-\frac{1}{2}} (x^3 + 1)' \right\} + 2x (x^3 + 1)^{\frac{1}{2}}$$

$$= x^2 \left\{ \frac{1}{2} (x^3 + 1)^{-\frac{1}{2}} \times 3x^2 \right\} + 2x (x^3 + 1)^{\frac{1}{2}} \quad (*)$$

$$= x^2 \left\{ \frac{3x^2}{2} \cdot \frac{1}{(x^3 + 1)^{\frac{1}{2}}} \right\} + 2x (x^3 + 1)^{\frac{1}{2}}$$

$$\therefore \quad \frac{dy}{dx} = \frac{3x^4}{2 (x^3 + 1)^{\frac{1}{2}}} + 2x (x^3 + 1)^{\frac{1}{2}}$$

Although this answer is satisfactory, a much tidier answer can be derived by factorising at line (*). This gives

$$\frac{dy}{dx} = (x^3 + 1)^{-\frac{1}{2}} \left\{ \frac{3x^4}{2} + 2x (x^3 + 1) \right\}$$

$$= (x^3 + 1)^{-\frac{1}{2}} \left\{ \frac{3x^4 + 4x^4 + 4x}{2} \right\}$$

$$= (x^3 + 1)^{-\frac{1}{2}} \left\{ \frac{7x^4 + 4x}{2} \right\}$$

$$= \frac{7x^4 + 4x}{2\sqrt{x^3 + 1}}$$

$$\therefore \quad \frac{dy}{dx} = \frac{x (7x^3 + 4)}{2\sqrt{x^3 + 1}}$$

11 Implicit differentiation

The function $y = x^2 + 2$ is an example of an explicit function. In other words, the variable y is written explicitly in terms of x.

Some functions are not expressed in the form $y = f(x)$, for example $x^3 + xy - y^3 = 1$. This is an example of an implicit function. In this case, it cannot be manipulated and expressed in the explicit form $y = f(x)$, meaning that a different technique is needed to differentiate such functions.

To find $\frac{dy}{dx}$ when the function is expressed implicitly, each term is differentiated with respect to x and the resulting expression is rearranged for $\frac{dy}{dx}$.

Example

Given the function $x^2 + y^3 - y = 4$, find $\frac{dy}{dx}$.

Solution

Differentiating each term with respect to x gives

$$\frac{d}{dx}(x^2) + \frac{d}{dx}(y^3) - \frac{d}{dx}(y) = \frac{d}{dx}(4)$$

i.e. $\quad 2x + 3y^2\frac{dy}{dx} - 1\frac{dy}{dx} = 0$

Rearranging for $\frac{dy}{dx}$

$$\frac{dy}{dx}(3y^2 - 1) = -2x$$

$$\therefore \quad \frac{dy}{dx} = \frac{-2x}{3y^2 - 1} = \frac{2x}{1 - 3y^2}$$

The detail involved in differentiating y^3 with respect to x:

$$\frac{d}{dx}(y^3) = \frac{d}{dy}(y^3) \times \frac{dy}{dx} \text{ (by the chain rule)}$$

$$= 3y^2\frac{dy}{dx}$$

In some cases, the implicit function involves a product.

Example

Find the gradient of the curve given by $x^2y - y^2 = 3$ at the point $P(2, 1)$. Hence find the equation of the normal to the curve at P.

Solution

Differentiating each term with respect to x, and using the product rule on the first term, gives

$$\left(x^2\frac{d(y)}{dx} + y\frac{d(x^2)}{dx}\right) - \frac{d(y^2)}{dx} = \frac{d(3)}{dx}$$

i.e. $\quad x^2\frac{dy}{dx} + 2xy - 2y\frac{dy}{dx} = 0$

$$\therefore \quad \frac{dy}{dx}(x^2 - 2y) = -2xy$$

$$\therefore \quad \frac{dy}{dx} = \frac{-2xy}{x^2 - 2y}$$

At $P(2, 1)$: $\frac{dy}{dx} = -\frac{2(2)(1)}{(2)^2 - 2(1)} = -\frac{4}{2} = -2.$

The gradient of the curve at P is -2.

Therefore, the gradient of the normal at P is $\frac{-1}{(-2)} = \frac{1}{2}$.

The equation of the normal is given by $y = \frac{1}{2}x + c$. Since the normal passes through $P(2, 1)$ we have

$$1 = \frac{1}{2}(2) + c$$

$$\therefore \quad c = 0$$

The equation of the normal to the curve at P is $y = \frac{1}{2}x$.

12 *Parametric differentiation*

In some cases, a function is defined by expressing both y and x in terms of a third variable, usually t. This third variable is known as a parametric. Such equations are called parametric equations.

To find $\dfrac{dy}{dx}$ when a function is expressed parametrically, each of the functions y and x are differentiated with respect to the third variable and the chain rule is used to find $\dfrac{dy}{dx}$.

Example

A curve is defined parametrically by $x = t^2$, $y = t^3 + 1$. Find

(i) the gradient of the curve at the point $(1, 0)$

(ii) $\dfrac{d^2y}{dx^2}$

Solution

(i) The gradient is given by $\dfrac{dy}{dx}$.

   If $x = t^2$, then $\dfrac{dx}{dt} = 2t$.

   If $y = t^3 + 1$, then $\dfrac{dy}{dt} = 3t^2$.

   By the chain rule,

   $$\frac{dy}{dx} = \frac{dy}{dt} \times \frac{dt}{dx}$$

   $$= 3t^2 \times \frac{1}{2t}$$

   $$\therefore \quad \frac{dy}{dx} = \frac{3t}{2}$$

   At the point $(1, 0)$, $t = -1$. Therefore, the gradient of the curve at $(1, 0)$ is given by

   $$\frac{dy}{dx} = \frac{3(-1)}{2} = -\frac{3}{2}$$

(ii) In order to find the second derivative, the first derivative is differentiated with respect to x, giving

   $$\frac{d^2y}{dx^2} = \frac{d\left(\frac{3t}{2}\right)}{dx} = \frac{d\left(\frac{3t}{2}\right)}{dt} \times \frac{dt}{dx}, \text{ by the chain rule}$$

   $$= \frac{3}{2} \times \frac{1}{2t}$$

   $$\therefore \quad \frac{d^2y}{dx^2} = \frac{3}{4t}$$

Example

A curve is defined parametrically by $x = 3\cos t$, $y = 3\sin t$. Find $\dfrac{dy}{dx}$.

Determine the Cartesian equation of the curve.

Solution

If $x = 3\cos t$, then $\dfrac{dx}{dt} = -3\sin t$

If $y = 3\sin t$, then $\dfrac{dy}{dt} = 3\cos t$

By the chain rule

$$\frac{dy}{dx} = \frac{dy}{dt} \cdot \frac{dt}{dx}$$

$$= 3\cos t \cdot \frac{1}{(-3\sin t)}$$

$$\therefore \quad \frac{dy}{dx} = -\cot t$$

To determine the Cartesian equation, eliminate the parameter t using the identity $\sin^2\theta + \cos^2\theta \equiv 1$.

Since $x = 3\cos t$ and $y = 3\sin t$,

$$x^2 + y^2 = 9\cos^2 t + 9\sin^2 t$$

$$= 9(\cos^2 t + \sin^2 t)$$

$$\therefore \quad x^2 + y^2 = 9$$

This is the Cartesian equation of the curve. This is the equation of a circle centred at the origin with a radius of 3.

Key points

- The chain rule states that if y is a function of u and u is a function of x, then

$$\frac{dy}{dx} = \frac{dy}{du} \cdot \frac{du}{dx}$$

- If $y = f(g(x))$ then $\dfrac{dy}{dx} = f'(g(x))g'(x)$ by the chain rule.

  This is a very useful form and enables easy differentiation of composite functions.

- If $y = \sec x$, then $\dfrac{dy}{dx} = \tan x \sec x$.

- If $y = \operatorname{cosec} x$, then $\dfrac{dy}{dx} = -\cot x \operatorname{cosec} x$.

- If $y = \cot x$, then $\dfrac{dy}{dx} = -\operatorname{cosec}^2 x$.

- If $y = \sin^{-1} x$, then $\dfrac{dy}{dx} = \dfrac{1}{\sqrt{1 - x^2}}$.

- If $y = \cos^{-1} x$, then $\dfrac{dy}{dx} = \dfrac{-1}{\sqrt{1 - x^2}}$.

- If $y = \tan^{-1}x$, then $\dfrac{dy}{dx} = \dfrac{1}{1 + x^2}$.

- The product rule states that if $y = u \cdot v$, then

$$\frac{dy}{dx} = u\frac{dv}{dx} + v\frac{du}{dx}$$

- The quotient rule states that if $y = \dfrac{u}{v}$, then

$$\frac{dy}{dx} = \frac{v\dfrac{du}{dx} - u\dfrac{dv}{dx}}{v^2}$$

- Given an implicit function, $\dfrac{dy}{dx}$ can be found by differentiating each term with respect to x and then manipulating the resulting expression to obtain $\dfrac{dy}{dx}$ as the subject.

- Given parametric equations, to find $\dfrac{dy}{dx}$, differentiate each of the functions y and x with respect to the third variable and use the chain rule.

13 Applications

13.1 MAXIMUM, MINIMUM AND POINTS OF INFLEXION

- All points on a curve at which the gradient is zero, i.e. $\dfrac{dy}{dx} = 0$, are called **stationary points**.

- There are three types of stationary points; these are shown below.

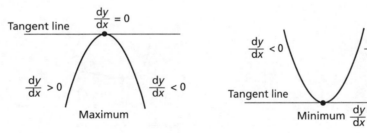

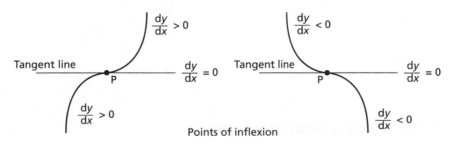

- There is another type of 'point of inflexion', namely one at which the gradient is non-zero at P. In this case, the point of inflexion is not a stationary point.

> **Example**
>
> Find the coordinates of the stationary point on the curve $y = \dfrac{x}{\ln x}$ and determine its nature. Sketch the curve.

TOPIC 8 Calculus I: differentiation

Solution

If $y = \dfrac{x}{\ln x}$, then using the quotient rule gives

$$\frac{dy}{dx} = \frac{\ln x - x \times \frac{1}{x}}{(\ln x)^2}$$

$$= \frac{\ln x - 1}{(\ln x)^2}$$

At a stationary point, $\dfrac{dy}{dx} = 0$. Therefore

$$\ln x - 1 = 0$$

$\therefore \qquad \ln x = 1$

$\therefore \qquad x = e$

When $x = e$, $y = \dfrac{e}{\ln e} = e$. The coordinates of the stationary point are (e, e).

In order to determine the nature of the stationary point, we check the gradient $\left(\dfrac{dy}{dx}\right)$ each side of the point. For (e, e),

x	2	3
$\dfrac{dy}{dx}$	$-ve$	$+ve$

The stationary point (e, e) is a minimum.

Sketching the curve gives

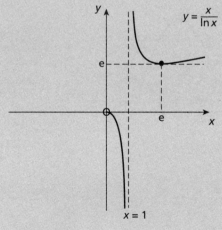

13.2 SECOND DERIVATIVE TESTS

- At a maximum, $\dfrac{dy}{dx} = 0$ and $\dfrac{d^2y}{dx^2} < 0$.

- At a minimum $\dfrac{dy}{dx} = 0$ and $\dfrac{d^2y}{dx^2} > 0$.

- At a point of inflexion, $\dfrac{d^2y}{dx^2} = 0$ and the gradient has the same sign either side of the point. This gradient test is necessary because $\dfrac{d^2y}{dx^2}$ can be zero at a maximum or minimum.

Note: $\dfrac{dy}{dx}$ may or may not be zero at a point of inflexion.

Example

Find the coordinates of the stationary point on the curve $y = xe^x$ and, using the second derivative, determine its nature. Determine the coordinates of the point of inflexion on the curve, which is not a stationary point. Sketch the curve.

Solution

If $y = xe^x$, then using the product rule, $\dfrac{dy}{dx} = xe^x + e^x$. At a stationary point, $\dfrac{dy}{dx} = 0$, giving

$$xe^x + e^x = 0$$

$$e^x(x + 1) = 0$$

$$\therefore \qquad x = -1 \quad \text{(note: } e^x > 0 \text{ for all } x\text{)}$$

When $x = -1$: $y = (-1)e^{-1} = -e^{-1}$. The coordinates of the stationary point are $\left(-1, -\dfrac{1}{e}\right)$.

To determine its nature, we find the second derivative, which gives

$$\frac{d^2y}{dx^2} = (xe^x + e^x) + e^x = xe^x + 2e^x$$

Evaluating the second derivative when $x = -1$ gives

$$\frac{d^2y}{dx^2} = -e^{-1} + 2e^{-1} = e^{-1} > 0 \Rightarrow \text{minimum}$$

Therefore, the stationary point $\left(-1, -\dfrac{1}{e}\right)$ is a minimum.

To find the point of inflexion that is not a stationary point, we need to solve $\dfrac{d^2y}{dx^2} = 0$ and investigate the gradient either side of the point. This gives

$$xe^x + 2e^x = 0$$

$$e^x(x + 2) = 0$$

$$\therefore \qquad x = -2 \quad \text{(note: } e^x > 0 \text{ for all } x\text{)}$$

When $x = -2$: $y = -2e^{-2}$.

To check that this is a stationary point, we examine the gradient either side of $x = -2$.

For $(-2, -2e^{-2})$:

x	-3	-2	$-\dfrac{3}{2}$
$\dfrac{dy}{dx}$	$-2e^{-3}$ negative		$-\dfrac{1}{2}e^{-\frac{3}{2}}$ negative

In other words, we have

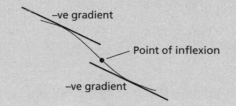

−ve gradient

Point of inflexion

−ve gradient

Sketching the curve gives

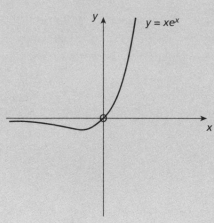

$y = xe^x$

13.3 PRACTICAL EXAMPLES

The techniques of determining maximum and minimum values are sometimes very useful in practical situations.

Example

A rectangular sheet of metal measures 20 cm by 15 cm. Equal squares of side x cm are cut from two of the corners, as shown below. The resulting piece of metal is shaped to form the tray of a shovel. Find the value of x if the volume of the tray is a maximum. Determine the maximum volume.

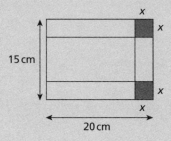

Solution

The volume of the resulting tray is given by

$$V = x (20 - x) (15 - 2x)$$

$$\therefore \quad V = 2x^3 - 55x^2 + 300x$$

The maximum volume occurs when $\dfrac{\mathrm{d}V}{\mathrm{d}x} = 0$. Differentiating and solving gives

$$\frac{\mathrm{d}V}{\mathrm{d}x} = 6x^2 - 110x + 300$$

i.e. $\quad 6x^2 - 110x + 300 = 0$

$\quad\quad 2(3x^2 - 55x + 150) = 0$

$\quad\quad 2(3x-10)(x - 15) = 0$

$\therefore \quad x = \dfrac{10}{3}$ or $x = 15$

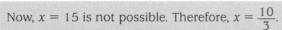

Now, $x = 15$ is not possible. Therefore, $x = \dfrac{10}{3}$.

We must check that this value of x corresponds to a maximum. The second derivative is given by

$$\dfrac{d^2V}{dx^2} = 12x - 110$$

When $x = \dfrac{10}{3}$, $\dfrac{d^2V}{dx^2} = 12\left(\dfrac{10}{3}\right) - 110 = -70 \; < 0 \Rightarrow$ maximum by the second derivative test.

Maximum volume, V_{max}, is found by substituting $x = \dfrac{10}{3}$ into $V = x(20 - x)(15 - x)$. This gives

$$V_{max} = \dfrac{10}{3} \cdot \dfrac{50}{3} \cdot \dfrac{25}{3}$$

$$\therefore \quad V_{max} = 462\dfrac{26}{27} \, \text{cm}^3$$

13.4 RATES OF CHANGE

- The derivative $\dfrac{dy}{dx}$ is called the rate of change of y with respect to x.

Many practical situations involve related changes in variables. For example, in mechanics, the rate of change of displacement with respect to time, $\dfrac{ds}{dt}$, denotes the velocity.

Example

The radius of a sphere is increasing at a rate of $0.1 \, \text{cm s}^{-1}$. Find
(i) the rate of increase of the volume
(ii) the rate of increase of the surface area, when this radius is $4 \, \text{cm}$

Solution

(i) We know that $V = \dfrac{4}{3}\pi r^3$ is the formula connecting volume and radius. Now, $\dfrac{dV}{dt}$ is the rate of change of volume with respect to time. Differentiating with respect to t gives

$$\dfrac{dV}{dt} = \dfrac{d}{dr}\left(\dfrac{4}{3}\pi r^3\right) \cdot \dfrac{dr}{dt}$$

$$= 4\pi r^2 \cdot \dfrac{dr}{dt}$$

Now, $\dfrac{dr}{dt} = 0.1 \, \text{cm s}^{-1}$ and $r = 4 \, \text{cm}$. Therefore,

$$\dfrac{dV}{dt} = 4\pi \, (4)^2 \, (0.1)$$

$$\therefore \quad \dfrac{dV}{dt} \approx 20.1$$

The rate of increase of the volume when the radius is $4 \, \text{cm}$ is approximately $20.1 \, \text{cm}^3 \text{s}^{-1}$.

(ii) We know that $S = 4\pi r^2$ is the formula connecting surface area and radius. Differentiating with respect to t gives

$$\frac{dS}{dt} = \frac{d}{dr}\,(4\pi r^2)\cdot \frac{dr}{dt}$$

$$= 8\pi r \cdot \frac{dr}{dt}$$

Now, $\dfrac{dr}{dt} = 0.1\,\text{cm}\,\text{s}^{-1}$ and $r = 4\,\text{cm}$. Therefore,

$$\frac{dS}{dt} = 8\pi\,(4)\,(0.1)$$

$$\therefore \quad \frac{dS}{dt} \approx 10.1$$

The rate of increase of the surface area when the radius is 4 cm is approximately $10.1\,\text{cm}^2\,\text{s}^{-1}$.

13.5   SMALL INCREMENTS

- If y and x are related quantities we know from the definition of first derivative that

$$\frac{dy}{dx} = \lim_{\delta x \to 0} \frac{\delta y}{\delta x}$$

where δy and δx are small changes.

If δx is small enough

$$\frac{\delta y}{\delta x} \approx \frac{dy}{dx}$$

i.e. $\delta y \approx \dfrac{dy}{dx}\delta x$

Example

The radius of a circular oil slick increases from 20 m to 20.3 m. Find the approximate increase in its area.

Solution

We know that $A = \pi r^2$, where A is the area of circular oil slick of radius r.

Now, $\delta A \approx \dfrac{dA}{dr}\delta r = 2\pi r \delta r$. The original radius is given as 20 m and the increase δr is given as 0.3 m. Therefore,

$$\delta A \approx 2\pi\,(20)\,(0.3) \approx 37.7$$

The approximate increase in area is $37.7\,\text{m}^2$.

Example

The radius of a sphere is increased by 3%. Find the approximate percentage increase in the volume.

Solution

We know that $V = \dfrac{4}{3}\pi r^3$, where V is the volume of a sphere with radius r. Now,

$$\delta V \approx \frac{dV}{dr}\delta r = 4\pi r^2 \delta r$$

The original radius is r and the increase δr is given as $0.03r$. Therefore,

$$\delta r \approx 4\pi r^2 \times 0.03r = 0.12\pi r^3$$

The percentage increase in V is given by

$$\frac{\delta V}{V} \times 100\% = \frac{0.12\pi r^3}{\left(\frac{4}{3}\pi r^3\right)} \times 100\%$$

$$= 9\%$$

The volume increase is 9%.

TOPIC 9 Calculus II: integration

1 Integration of x^n and Ax^n

Integration is the reverse process of differentiation. In other words, given $\frac{dy}{dx}$, find the function y.

1.1 NOTATION

We use the symbol $\int$ (integral sign) to indicate the operation 'integrate'.

- We have the following result:

$$\int Ax^n \, dx = \frac{Ax^{n+1}}{n+1} + c \quad (n \neq -1)$$

The 'dx' indicates that the integration is with respect to the variable x.

The 'c' is the constant of integration.

Note: the integration process in this case can be summarised as 'add one to the power and divide by the new power', i.e. the reverse of differentiation.

- When the integrand comprises the sum and/or difference of a number of functions, integration can be performed on each term in turn.

$$\int f(x) \pm g(x) \, dx = \int f(x) \, dx \pm \int g(x) \, dx$$

- A constant multiplier can be taken outside the integral sign to simplify the integrand, i.e. $\int kf(x) \, dx = k \int f(x) \, dx$.

Example

Find

(i) $\int 2x^3 \, dx$

(ii) $\int \frac{1}{\sqrt{x}} \, dx$

(iii) $\int \left(1 + \sqrt{x}\right)^2 \, dx$

Solution

(i) $\int 2x^3 \, dx = 2 \int x^3 \, dx = 2 \times \frac{x^4}{4} + c = \frac{1}{2}x^4 + c$

(ii) $\int \frac{1}{\sqrt{x}} \, dx = \int x^{-\frac{1}{2}} \, dx = \frac{x^{\frac{1}{2}}}{\left(\frac{1}{2}\right)} + c = 2\sqrt{x} + c$

(iii) In this case, the brackets must be expanded so that the integrand is written in a standard form.

$$\int \left(1 + \sqrt{x}\right)^2 dx = \int \left(1 + \sqrt{x}\right)\left(1 + \sqrt{x}\right) dx$$

$$= \int \left(1 + 2\sqrt{x} + x\right) dx$$

$$= \int 1 \, dx + \int 2\sqrt{x} \, dx + \int x \, dx$$

$$= \int 1 \, dx + 2 \int x^{\frac{1}{2}} \, dx + \int x \, dx$$

$$= x + 2 \frac{x^{\frac{3}{2}}}{\left(\frac{3}{2}\right)} + \frac{x^2}{2} + c$$

$$= x + \frac{4}{3} x^{\frac{3}{2}} + \frac{x^2}{2} + c$$

2 Integration of e^{kx} and $\frac{1}{x}$

- $\int e^{kx} \, dx = \frac{1}{k} e^{kx} + c$

- $\int \frac{1}{x} \, dx = \ln x + c$

These two results can easily be confirmed by differentiating both $\frac{1}{k} e^{kx}$ and $\ln x$.

Example

Find

(i) $\int 3e^{2x} \, dx$

(ii) $\int \left(1 + \frac{1}{x}\right)^2 dx$

Solution

(i) $\int 3e^{2x} \, dx = 3 \int e^{2x} \, dx = 3 \times \frac{1}{2} e^{2x} + c = \frac{3}{2} e^{2x} + c$

(ii) $\int \left(1 + \frac{1}{x}\right)^2 dx = \int \left(1 + \frac{1}{x}\right)\left(1 + \frac{1}{x}\right) dx$

$$= \int \left(1 + \frac{2}{x} + \frac{1}{x^2}\right) dx$$

$$= \int 1.dx + \int \frac{2}{x} dx + \int \frac{1}{x^2} dx$$

$$= \int 1.dx + 2\int \frac{1}{x} dx + \int x^{-2} dx$$

$$= x + 2\ln x + \frac{x^{-1}}{(-1)} + c$$

$$\therefore \int \left(1 + \frac{1}{x}\right)^2 dx = x + 2\ln x - \frac{1}{x} + c$$

3 Integration of $\frac{f'(x)}{f(x)}$

The result that has been used in the previous example, namely $\int \frac{1}{x} dx = \ln x + c$, is a special case of a more general rule.

Generally,

$$\int \frac{f'(x)}{f(x)} dx = \ln(f(x)) + c$$

This is a powerful result and can be used in those cases where the differential of the denominator is the numerator *or* a constant multiple of the numerator.

Example

Find

(i) $\int \frac{1}{2x-1} dx$

(ii) $\int \frac{x+3}{x^2+6x} dx$

(iii) $\int \frac{\cos x}{\sin x} + 2 \, dx$

Solution

A useful technique is to rewrite the integral with the derivative of the denominator as the numerator. This then enables appropriate constants to be introduced, ensuring that the main integrand remains unchanged.

(i) $\int \frac{1}{2x-1} dx = \frac{1}{2} \int \frac{2}{2x-1} dx$

$\qquad\qquad\qquad = \frac{1}{2} \ln(2x-1) + c$

(ii) $\int \frac{x+3}{x^2+6x} dx = \int \frac{1}{2} \frac{(2x+6)}{x^2+6x} dx$

$\qquad\qquad\qquad = \frac{1}{2} \int \frac{2x+6}{x^2+6x} dx$

$\qquad\qquad\qquad = \frac{1}{2} \ln(x^2+6x) + c$

(iii) $\int \frac{\cos x}{\sin x + 2} dx = \ln(\sin x + 2) + c$

4 Integration of trigonometric functions

There are a number of standard trigonometric integrals that are based on standard differentials.

4.1 STANDARD RESULTS

- $\int \sin ax \, dx = -\frac{1}{a}\cos ax + c$

- $\int \cos ax \, dx = \frac{1}{a}\sin ax + c$

- $\int \sec^2 ax \, dx = \frac{1}{a}\tan ax + c$

4.2 FURTHER RESULTS

- $\int \operatorname{cosec}^2 ax \, dx = -\frac{1}{a}\cot ax + c$

- $\int \cot ax \operatorname{cosec} ax \, dx = -\frac{1}{a}\operatorname{cosec} ax + c$

- $\int \tan ax \sec ax \, dx = \frac{1}{a}\sec ax + c$

Example

Find

(i) $\int \sin 5x \, dx$

(ii) $\int 3\operatorname{cosec}^2 2x \, dx$

(iii) $\int 2\tan\left(\frac{x}{2}\right)\sec\left(\frac{x}{2}\right) dx$

Solution

(i) $\int \sin 5x \, dx = -\frac{1}{5}\cos 5x + c$

(ii) $\int 3\operatorname{cosec}^2 2x \, dx = 3\int \operatorname{cosec}^2 2x \, dx$

$$= 3\left(-\frac{1}{2}\cot 2x\right) + c$$

$$= -\frac{3}{2}\cot 2x + c$$

(iii) $\int 2\tan\left(\frac{x}{2}\right)\sec\left(\frac{x}{2}\right) dx = 2\int \tan\left(\frac{x}{2}\right)\sec\left(\frac{x}{2}\right) dx$

$$= 2\left(\frac{1}{\left(\frac{1}{2}\right)}\sec\left(\frac{x}{2}\right)\right) + c$$

$$= 4\sec\left(\frac{x}{2}\right) + c$$

Example

Find

(i) $\int \tan x \, dx$

(ii) $\int \cot x \, dx$

Solution

(i) $\int \tan x \, dx = \int \dfrac{\sin x}{\cos x} \, dx$

Now, using the result for $\int \dfrac{f'(x)}{f(x)} \, dx$ we have

$$-\int -\dfrac{\sin x}{\cos x} \, dx = -\ln(\cos x) + c$$

This can be manipulated further using properties of logarithms, since

$$-\ln(\cos x) = \ln(\cos x)^{-1} = \ln\left(\dfrac{1}{\cos x}\right) = \ln(\sec x)$$

(ii) $\int \cot x \, dx = \int \dfrac{\cos x}{\sin x} \, dx = \ln(\sin x) + c$

4.3 INTEGRATION OF $\sin^2 x$, $\cos^2 x$ AND $\tan^2 x$

Some trigonometric integrals require manipulation using trigonometric identities before the integration can be performed. Three common ones are $\sin^2 x$, $\cos^2 x$ and $\tan^2 x$.

- In order to find $\int \sin^2 x \, dx$, we use the identity $\cos 2x \equiv 1 - 2\sin^2 x$.
- In order to find $\int \cos^2 x \, dx$, we use the identity $\cos 2x \equiv 2\cos^2 x - 1$.
- In order to find $\int \tan^2 x \, dx$, we use the identity $\sec^2 x \equiv \tan^2 x + 1$.

Example

Find $\int \sin^2 x \, dx$.

Solution

Using $\cos 2x \equiv 1 - 2\sin^2 x$ and rearranging gives $\sin^2 x \equiv \dfrac{1}{2} - \dfrac{\cos 2x}{2}$. We have

$$\int \sin^2 x \, dx = \int \left(\dfrac{1}{2} - \dfrac{\cos 2x}{2}\right) dx$$

$$= \int \dfrac{1}{2} \, dx - \int \dfrac{\cos 2x}{2} \, dx$$

$$= \dfrac{1}{2}x - \dfrac{1}{2} \cdot \dfrac{\sin 2x}{2} + c$$

$$= \dfrac{x}{2} - \dfrac{\sin 2x}{4} + c$$

Others solutions are left to the reader.

5 _Integration using partial fractions_

We have seen how to integrate an algebraic fraction, which comprises a function in the denominator and its derivative as the numerator. However, an algebraic fraction such as $\dfrac{3x-1}{x(x-1)}$ cannot be integrated in this way. Since the denominator comprises a product of linear factors, the fraction can be split into its partial fractions and then each term integrated.

Example

Find $\int \dfrac{3x-1}{x\,(x-1)}\,dx$.

Solution

Using partial fraction methods, we see that $\dfrac{3x-1}{x\,(x-1)} = \dfrac{1}{x} + \dfrac{2}{x-1}$. Therefore,

$$\int \frac{3x-1}{x\,(x-1)}\,dx = \int \left(\frac{1}{x} + \frac{2}{x-1}\right) dx$$

$$= \int \frac{1}{x}\,dx + \int \frac{2}{x-1}\,dx$$

$$= \int \frac{1}{x}\,dx + 2\int \frac{1}{x-1}\,dx$$

$$= \ln x + 2\ln (x-1) + c$$

Further manipulation of the logarithmic term gives

$$\int \frac{3x-1}{x\,(x-1)}\,dx = \ln x + \ln (x-1)^2 + c$$

$$= \ln (x\,(x-1)^2) + c$$

Example

Find $\int \dfrac{x^2}{x+1}\,dx$.

Solution

In this case the integrand is an improper fraction (the degree of the numerator is greater than the degree of the denominator). Using partial fraction methods, we see that

$$\frac{x^2}{x+1} = x - 1 + \frac{1}{x+1}$$

Therefore,

$$\int \frac{x^2}{x+1}\,dx = \int \left(x - 1 + \frac{1}{x+1}\right) dx$$

$$= \int x\,dx - \int 1\,dx + \int \frac{1}{x+1}\,dx$$

$$= \frac{x^2}{2} - x + \ln (x+1) + c$$

6 Integration of $f'(x)\,[f(x)]^n$

This is a useful form to recognise. It is the reverse of the chain rule used for differentiating composite functions.

- $\int f'(x)\,[f(x)]^n\,dx = \dfrac{[f(x)]^{n+1}}{n+1} + c$

For example, the integral $\int 2x\,(x^2+1)^4\,dx$ is of the required form, since $f(x) = (x^2+1)$ and $f'(x) = 2x$. Therefore

$$\int 2x\,(x^2+1)^4\,dx = \frac{(x^2+1)^5}{5} + c$$

Important point

It is important to remember that constants as multipliers do not change the form. For example, the integral $\int x\,(x^2+1)^4\,dx$ is also of the required form, since it can be written as $\frac{1}{2}\int 2x\,(x^2+1)^4\,dx$. Therefore,

$$\int x\,(x^2+1)^4\,dx = \frac{1}{2}\int 2x\,(x^2+1)^4\,dx = \frac{1}{2}\frac{(x^2+1)^5}{5} + c$$

$$= \frac{(x^2+1)^5}{10} + c$$

Example

Find

(i) $\displaystyle\int \frac{x}{\sqrt{x^2-3}}\,dx$

(ii) $\displaystyle\int 3x\sin x^2\,dx$

(iii) $\displaystyle\int x e x^2\,dx$

Solution

(i) $\displaystyle\int x(x^2-3)^{-\frac{1}{2}}\,dx = \frac{1}{2}\int 2x(x^2-3)^{-\frac{1}{2}}\,dx$, i.e. the required form

$$= \frac{1}{2}\frac{(x^2-3)^{\frac{1}{2}}}{\left(\frac{1}{2}\right)} + c$$

$$= \sqrt{x^2-3} + c$$

(ii) $\displaystyle\int 3x\sin x^2\,dx = \frac{3}{2}\int 2x\sin x^2\,dx$, i.e. the required form

$$= \frac{3}{2}\,(-\cos x^2) + c$$

$$= -\frac{3}{2}\cos x^2 + c$$

(iii) $\displaystyle\int x e x^2\,dx = \frac{1}{2}\int 2x e x^2\,dx$

$$= \frac{1}{2}e x^2 + c$$

7   *Integrals* $\int \frac{1}{\sqrt{a^2 - x^2}}$ dx *and* $\int \frac{1}{a^2 + x^2}$ dx

- $\int \dfrac{1}{\sqrt{a^2 - x^2}} \, dx = \sin^{-1}\left(\dfrac{x}{a}\right) + c$

- $\int \dfrac{1}{a^2 + x^2} \, dx = \dfrac{1}{a} \tan^{-1}\left(\dfrac{x}{a}\right) + c$

Note: these are clearly derived from the derivatives of $\sin^{-1} x$ and $\tan^{-1} x$.

Example

Find

(i) $\displaystyle\int \frac{1}{\sqrt{25 - x^2}} \, dx$

(ii) $\displaystyle\int \frac{1}{4 + 3x^2} \, dx$

Solution

(i) Using the result given,

$$\int \frac{1}{\sqrt{25 - x^2}} \, dx = \int \frac{1}{\sqrt{5^2 - x^2}} \, dx$$

$$= \sin^{-1}\left(\frac{x}{5}\right) + c$$

(ii) To use the result for inverse tangent, a factor of 3 needs to be taken out of the denominator. This gives

$$\int \frac{1}{4 + 3x^2} \, dx = \int \frac{1}{3\left(\frac{4}{3} + x^2\right)} \, dx$$

$$= \frac{1}{3} \int \frac{1}{\left(\frac{2}{\sqrt{3}}\right)^2 + x^2} \, dx$$

$$= \frac{1}{3} \times \frac{1}{\left(\frac{2}{\sqrt{3}}\right)} \tan^{-1}\left(\frac{x}{\left(\frac{2}{\sqrt{3}}\right)}\right) + c$$

$$\therefore \quad \int \frac{1}{4 + 3x^2} \, dx = \frac{\sqrt{3}}{6} \tan^{-1}\left(\frac{x\sqrt{3}}{2}\right) + c$$

8   *Integration by substitution*

Sometimes it is necessary to make a substitution and change the variable of the integrand.

Example

By making the substitution $u = x + 2$, find $\int x\sqrt{x + 2}\,dx$.

Solution

If $u = x + 2$, then $\dfrac{du}{dx} = 1$ and $x = u - 2$.

Substituting gives

$$I = \int x\sqrt{x + 2}\,dx = \int (u - 2)u^{\frac{1}{2}}\frac{dx}{du}\,du$$

$$= \int u^{\frac{1}{2}}(u - 2)\,du, \text{ since } \frac{dx}{du} = 1$$

$$= \int \left(u^{\frac{3}{2}} - 2u^{\frac{1}{2}}\right)du$$

$$= \frac{u^{\frac{5}{2}}}{\left(\frac{5}{2}\right)} - \frac{2u^{\frac{3}{2}}}{\left(\frac{3}{2}\right)} + c$$

$$\therefore \qquad I = \frac{2u^{\frac{5}{2}}}{5} - \frac{4u^{\frac{3}{2}}}{3} + c$$

Since $u = x + 2$, we have $I = \dfrac{2}{5}(x + 2)^{\frac{5}{2}} - \dfrac{4}{3}(x + 2)^{\frac{3}{2}} + c$.

Further algebraic manipulation gives

$$I = 2(x + 2)^{\frac{3}{2}}\left\{\frac{1}{5}(x + 2) - \frac{2}{3}\right\} + c$$

$$= 2(x + 2)^{\frac{3}{2}}\left\{\frac{3x + 6 - 10}{15}\right\} + c$$

$$\therefore \qquad I = 2(x + 2)^{\frac{3}{2}}\left\{\frac{3x - 4}{15}\right\} + c$$

9   *Integration by parts*

This method is used to integrate the product of two functions and is given as

$$\int u \cdot \frac{dv}{dx}\,dx = uv - \int v \cdot \frac{du}{dx}\,dx$$

It is derived from the product rule

$$\frac{d}{dx}(uv) = u\frac{dv}{dx} + v\frac{du}{dx}$$

Integrating both sides with respect to x gives

$$uv = \int u \cdot \frac{dv}{dx}\,dx + \int v \cdot \frac{du}{dx}\,dx$$

$$\therefore \quad \int u \cdot \frac{dv}{dx}\,dx = uv - \int v \cdot \frac{du}{dx}\,dx$$

A more convenient way of remembering this is $\int u \cdot v' = uv - \int v \cdot u'$.

Example

Find $\int x \cos x \, dx$.

Solution

It is important to recognise that by letting $u = x$, $u' = 1$ and that this will result in a simpler integrand on the right-hand side ($\int v \cdot u'$).

Let $u = x$

$\therefore \quad u' = 1$

Let $v' = \cos x$

$\therefore \quad v = \sin x$

Therefore,

$$\int x \cos x \, dx = x \sin x - \int \sin x \cdot 1 \, dx$$

$$= x \sin x - (-\cos x) + c$$

$$\therefore \quad \int x \cos x \, dx = x \sin x + \cos x + c$$

Example

Find $\int x \ln x \, dx$.

Solution

In this case, if we let $u = x$, then $v' = \ln x$, but we do not know how to integrate $\ln x$ to find v.

Therefore, this is a case in which we let

$$u = \ln x$$

$$\therefore \quad u' = \frac{1}{x}$$

$$v' = x$$

$$\therefore \quad v = \frac{x^2}{2}$$

This gives

$$\int x \ln x \, dx = \frac{x^2}{2} \ln x - \int \frac{x^2}{2} \cdot \frac{1}{x} \, dx$$

$$= \frac{x^2}{2} \ln x - \frac{1}{2} \int x \, dx$$

$$= \frac{x^2}{2} \ln x - \frac{1}{2} \cdot \frac{x^2}{2} + c$$

$$\therefore \quad \int x \ln x \, dx = \frac{x^2}{2} \ln x - \frac{x^2}{4} + c$$

Key points

- $\int Ax^n dx = \dfrac{Ax^{n+1}}{n+1} + c \quad (n \neq -1)$

  (Used when integrating polynomial expressions.)

- $\int e^{kx} dx = \dfrac{1}{k} e^{kx} + c \qquad$ (k constant)

- $\int \dfrac{1}{x} dx = \ln x + c$

- $\int \dfrac{f'(x)}{f(x)} dx = \ln(f(x)) + c$

  (Remember, this still applies if the numerator is a multiple of $f'(x)$.)

- $\int \sin ax \, dx = -\dfrac{1}{a} \cos ax + c$

- $\int \cos ax \, dx = \dfrac{1}{a} \sin ax + c$

- $\int \sec^2 ax \, dx = \dfrac{1}{a} \tan ax + c$

- To find $\int \sin^2 x \, dx$, use the identity $\cos 2x \equiv 1 - 2\sin^2 x$.

- To find $\int \cos^2 x \, dx$, use the identity $\cos 2x \equiv 2\cos^2 x - 1$.

- To find $\int \tan^2 x \, dx$, use the identity $\sec^2 x \equiv \tan^2 x + 1$.

- Polynomial quotients may be split into partial fractions and integrated term by term. Look out for a factorising denominator term.

- $\int f'(x)[f(x)]^n dx = \dfrac{[f(x)]^{n+1}}{n+1} + c$

  This is a very useful result if the required form is identified. Look for the differential of the 'main' term outside the bracket.

- $\int \dfrac{1}{\sqrt{a^2 - x^2}} dx = \sin^{-1}\left(\dfrac{x}{a}\right) + c$

- $\int \dfrac{1}{a^2 + x^2} dx = \dfrac{1}{a} \tan^{-1}\left(\dfrac{x}{a}\right) + c$

- Some integrals require a substitution and, usually, examination questions identify such substitutions. The substitution should transform the integrand into something much simpler.

- $\int u.v' = uv - \int v.u'$ (integration by parts). Use this on products of functions such as $x\sin x$, xe^x, $(x+1)\ln x$.

10 _Definite integrals_

The integral $\int_a^b f(x)\,dx$ is known as a **definite integral**, because the limits of integration ($x = a$, $x = b$) are known and it will give a definite answer. To evaluate a definite integral, first integrate and then use the limits of integration. For example,

$$\int_1^2 3x^2\,dx = \left[x^3 + c\right]_1^2$$

$$= \left[(2)^3 + c\right] - \left[(1)^3 + c\right]$$

$$= 8 - 1$$

$$= 7$$

Note: (i) the use of square brackets, (ii) the constants of integration cancel and so we do not usually include them when working with definite integrals.

Important points

- **Evaluating definite integrals using the substitution method.** When the method of substitution is used to determine an integral, the variable is changed. For example, the solution may involve letting $u = 2x + 1$, i.e. the variable is changed from x to u. When dealing with definite integrals, the limits must also be changed to match the 'new' variable.

Example

By using the substitution $u = 5 - x$, evaluate $\int_1^2 \dfrac{x}{5 - x}\,dx$.

Solution

If $u = 5 - x$, then $\dfrac{du}{dx} = -1$ and $x = 5 - u$. Substituting gives

$$\int \frac{x}{5 - x}\,dx = \int \frac{5 - u}{u}\,(-1)\,du$$

$$= \int \frac{u - 5}{u}\,du$$

$$= \int 1 - \frac{5}{u}\,du$$

At this stage, the limits are not included.

The original limits are x limits, and we now need the corresponding u limits. When $x = 1$, $u = 5 - 1 = 4$; when $x = 2$, $u = 5 - 2 = 3$. Therefore, we have

$$\int_1^2 \frac{x}{5 - x}\,dx = \int_4^3 1 - \frac{5}{u}\,du$$

Even though the lower u limit is greater than the upper u limit, the 'new' limits must correspond to the original x limits.

Working with the integral involving the variable u gives

$$\int_4^3 1 - \frac{5}{u}\,du = \left[u - 5\ln u\right]_4^3$$

$$= (3 - 5\ln 3) - (4 - 5\ln 4)$$

$$= -1 - 5\ln 3 + 5\ln 4$$

$$= -1 - 5(\ln 3 - \ln 4)$$

$$\therefore \int_1^2 \frac{x}{5 - x}\,dx = -1 - 5\ln\left(\frac{3}{4}\right)$$

TOPIC 9 Calculus II: integration

- **Definite integrals involving trigonometric functions.** When evaluating definite integrals that involve trigonometric functions, the limits of integration are always in radians and are usually given as multiples of π.

Example

Evaluate $\displaystyle\int_0^{\frac{\pi}{3}} \cos x \, dx$.

Solution

We have

$$\int_0^{\frac{\pi}{3}} \cos x \, dx = \Big[\sin x \Big]_0^{\frac{\pi}{3}}$$

$$= \sin\frac{\pi}{3} - \sin 0$$

$$\therefore \quad \int_0^{\frac{\pi}{3}} \cos x \, dx = \frac{\sqrt{3}}{2}$$

- **Definite integrals involving logarithms.** We know that

$$\int \frac{1}{x} \, dx = \ln x + c \text{ and } \int \frac{f'(x)}{f(x)} \, dx = \ln(f(x)) + c$$

when dealing with indefinite integrals. When dealing with definite integrals, it is usual practice to use the following results

$$\int \frac{1}{x} \, dx = \ln|x| + c \text{ and } \int \frac{f'(x)}{f(x)} \, dx = \ln|f(x)| + c$$

These two results take account of the fact that the log function is not defined for negative values.

Generally, when evaluating definite integrals, the interval of integration should not include any discontinuities.

For example, it would not make sense to write $\displaystyle\int_{-1}^{2} \frac{1}{x} \, dx$, since $\frac{1}{x}$ is not defined when $x = 0$.

Example

Evaluate $\displaystyle\int_1^2 \frac{1}{1 - 2x} \, dx$.

Solution

Rewriting, so that the derivative of the denominator is the numerator,

$$\int_1^2 \frac{1}{1 - 2x} \, dx = -\frac{1}{2} \int_1^2 \frac{-2}{1 - 2x} \, dx$$

$$= -\frac{1}{2} \Big[\ln|1 - 2x| + c \Big]_1^2$$

$$= -\frac{1}{2} \{ \ln|-3| - \ln|-1| \}$$

$$= -\frac{1}{2} \ln 3$$

Notice that $\frac{1}{1 - 2x}$ is defined for $1 \le x \le 2$. The exceptional point is $x = \frac{1}{2}$, which lies outside the interval of integration.

11   *Applications*

11.1   AREA UNDER A CURVE

- The area A under a curve $f(x)$ between the ordinates $x = a$, $x = b$ and the x-axis is given by

$$A = \int_a^b f(x)\,dx$$

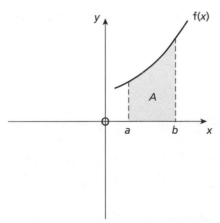

- If the area A lies above the x-axis, then the integral $\int_a^b f(x)\,dx$ will give a positive answer.

- If the area A lies below the x-axis, then the integral $\int_a^b f(x)\,dx$ will give a negative answer.

- Thus, the area is given by the absolute value.

In some cases, part of the area A lies below the x-axis, while part lies above. In such cases, the areas need to be considered separately.

Example

Find the area under the curve $y = \dfrac{1}{x}$ between $x = 1$ and $x = 2$.

Solution

A sketch shows that the required area lies entirely above the x-axis.

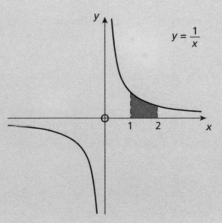

The area is given by

$$A = \int_1^2 \frac{1}{x}\,dx$$
$$= \Big[\ln|x|\Big]_1^2$$
$$= \ln 2 - \ln 1$$

$$\therefore \quad A = \ln 2$$

The required area is $\ln 2$.

> Very often exam questions require the answer to be left in terms of ln.

Example

Sketch the curve given by $y = x^3 - 4x^2 + x + 6$.

Find the area enclosed by the curve and the x-axis.

Solution

Factorising gives

$$x^3 - 4x^2 + x + 6 = (x - 2)(x - 3)(x + 1)$$

Therefore, the curve crosses the x-axis when $x = 2, 3$ and -1. Noting that $y = 6$ when $x = 0$, we have the following graph.

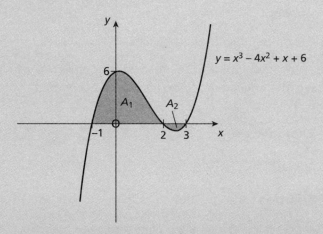

The required area is $A_1 + A_2$. Each area needs to be calculated separately, since A_2 lies below the x-axis.

$$\int_{-1}^2 (x^3 - 4x^2 + x + 6)\,dx = \left[\frac{x^4}{4} - \frac{4x^3}{3} + \frac{x^2}{2} + 6x\right]_{-1}^2$$

$$= \frac{22}{3} - \left(-\frac{47}{12}\right)$$

$$= \frac{45}{4}$$

$$\therefore \qquad\qquad A_1 = \frac{45}{4}$$

$$\int_2^3 (x^3 - 4x^2x + 6)\,dx = \left[\frac{x^4}{4} - \frac{4x^3}{3} + \frac{x^2}{2} + 6x\right]_2^3$$

$$= \frac{27}{4} - \left(\frac{22}{3}\right)$$

$$= -\frac{7}{12} \quad \text{(negative, as expected)}$$

$$\therefore \qquad A_2 = \frac{7}{12}$$

Therefore, the required area is given by

$$A_1 + A_2 = \frac{45}{4} + \frac{7}{12} = \frac{71}{6}$$

11.2 THE AREA BETWEEN TWO CURVES

The area A between two intersecting curves $f(x)$ and $g(x)$ is given by

$$A = \int_a^b [g(x) - f(x)]\,dx, \text{ where } g(x) \ge f(x) \text{ for } a \le x \le b$$

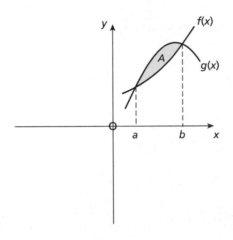

This result is very useful, since it accommodates those situations where part of the required area lies below the x-axis.

Example

Find the coordinates of the points of intersection of $y = 4x - x^2$ and $y = -2x$. Find the area enclosed by the curve and the line.

Solution

To find the x coordinates of the points of intersection, we solve the equation

$$4x - x^2 = -2x$$

i.e. $\quad x^2 - 6x = 0$

$\therefore \quad x(x - 6) = 0$

Solving gives $x = 0$ and $x = 6$.

When $x = 0$, $y = -2(0) = 0$

When $x = 6$, $y = -2(6) = -12$

The following sketch shows the required area, A.

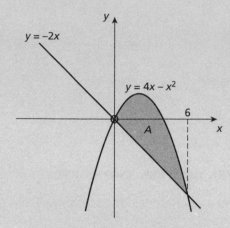

The area A is given by

$$A = \int_0^6 \left[(4x - x^2) - (-2x) \right] dx$$

$$= \int_0^6 (6x - x^2)\, dx$$

$$= \left[3x^2 - \frac{x^3}{3} \right]_0^6$$

$$= (108 - 72) - (0)$$

$$\therefore \quad A = 36$$

The required area is 36.

11.3 PARAMETRIC FORM

- If a curve is defined parametrically with x and y expressed in terms of a third variable t, then the area under such a curve is given by

$$\int_a^b y\, dx = \int_c^d y \frac{dx}{dt} dt$$

where c and d are the t-limits corresponding to the x-limits a and b.

Example

A curve is defined parametrically by the equations $x = t^2$, $y = t^2 - t$.

Sketch the curve for values of t in the interval $-2 \leq t \leq 2$.

Find the area under the section of curve defined for $1 \leq t \leq 2$.

11 *Applications*

Solution

The table of values is

t	-2	-1	0	1	2
x	4	1	0	1	4
y	6	2	0	0	2

The sketch is

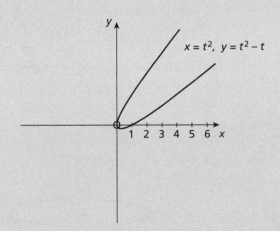

The required area A is given by

$$A = \int_1^2 y\frac{dx}{dt}\,dt$$

If $x = t^2$ then $\frac{dx}{dt} = 2t$. Therefore,

$$A = \int_1^2 (t^2 - t)\,2t\,dt$$

$$= \int_1^2 (2t^3 - 2t^2)\,dt$$

$$= 2\int_1^2 (t^3 - t^2)\,dt$$

$$= 2\left[\frac{t^4}{4} - \frac{t^3}{3}\right]_1^2$$

$$= 2\left[\left(4 - \frac{8}{3}\right) - \left(\frac{1}{4} - \frac{1}{3}\right)\right]$$

$$\therefore\quad A = \frac{17}{6}$$

The required area is $\frac{17}{6}$.

11.4 VOLUMES OF REVOLUTION

The volume, V, of the solid formed when the area enclosed by the curve $y = f(x)$, the x-axis and the ordinates $x = a$, $x = b$ is rotated through 2π radians about the x-axis is given by

$$V = \pi \int_a^b y^2\,dx$$

Exam Revision Notes

121

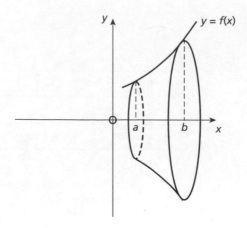

Similarly, the volume, V, of the solid formed by rotating an area through 2π radians about the y-axis is given by

$$V = \pi \int_a^b x^2 \, dy$$

where, in this case, a and b are y-limits.

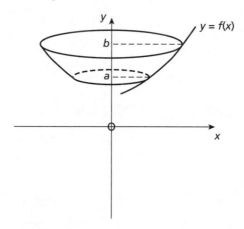

Example

Find the volume of the solid formed when the area between the curve $y = \frac{1}{x}$ and the x-axis from $x = 1$ to $x = 3$ is rotated through 2π radians about the x-axis.

Solution

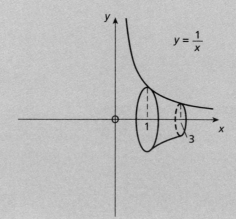

The volume is given by

$$V = \pi \int_1^3 \left(\frac{1}{x}\right)^2 dx$$

$$= \pi \int_1^3 x^{-2} dx$$

$$= \pi \left[\frac{x^{-1}}{(-1)}\right]_1^3$$

$$= \pi \left[-\frac{1}{x}\right]_1^3$$

$$= \pi \left\{-\frac{1}{3} - (-1)\right\}$$

$$\therefore \quad V = \frac{2\pi}{3}$$

The required volume is $\frac{2\pi}{3}$.

Example

Find the volume of the solid formed when the area between the curve $y = x^2 + 1$ and the y-axis from $y = 2$ to $y = 4$ is rotated through 2π radians about the y-axis.

Solution

The volume is given by

$$V = \pi \int_2^4 x^2 dy$$

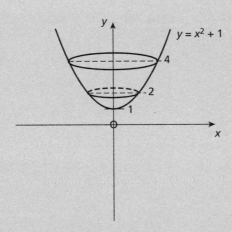

Now, since $y = x^2 + 1$, we have $x^2 = y - 1$. Therefore,

$$V = \pi \int_2^4 (y - 1) dy$$

$$= \pi \left[\frac{y^2}{2} - y\right]_2^4$$

$$= \pi \left\{(8 - 4) - (2 - 2)\right\}$$

$$\therefore \quad V = 4\pi$$

The required volume is 4π.

Key points

- Definite integrals involve limits of integration and give a definite answer. When dealing with definite integrals, use the following log results:

  - $\int \frac{1}{x}\mathrm{d}x = \ln|x| + c$

  - $\int \frac{f'(x)}{f(x)}\mathrm{d}x = \ln|f(x)| + c$

- $\int_a^b f(x)\mathrm{d}x$ represents the area under the curve $y = f(x)$ between $x = a$, $x = b$. When answering area questions, always sketch the curve and identify the area.

- In those cases where part of the required enclosed area lies below the x-axis, the area has to be calculated in two parts: first, the part above the x-axis and second, the part below the x-axis.

- $\int_a^b [g(x) - f(x)]\mathrm{d}x$ gives the area between two intersecting curves, $f(x)$ and $g(x)$, and takes account of any area that falls below the x-axis.

- If a curve is defined parametrically (third variable t, say), then the area under the curve is given by

  $$\int_c^d y\frac{\mathrm{d}x}{\mathrm{d}t}\,\mathrm{d}t$$

  where c and d are t-limits.

- $\pi \int_a^b y^2\mathrm{d}x$ represents the volume of the solid formed when the enclosed area is rotated through 2π radians about the x-axis (a and b are x-limits).

- $\pi \int_a^b x^2\mathrm{d}y$ represents the volume of the solid formed when the enclosed area is rotated through 2π radians about the y-axis (a and b are y-limits).

TOPIC 10 Calculus III: differential equations

1 First-order differential equations

An equation which involves only a first-order derivative is called a **first-order differential equation**.

For example, $3\dfrac{dy}{dx} + x = y$ is a first-order differential equation.

Differential equations of the form $\dfrac{dy}{dx} = f(x)$ can be solved by integrating term by term.

Example

Solve the differential equation $\dfrac{dy}{dx} = \cos x + 3x^2$, given that $y = 2$ when $x = 0$.

Solution

Integrating with respect to x gives

$$\int \frac{dy}{dx}dx = \int \cos x + 3x^2\,dx$$

$$\therefore \qquad y = \sin x + x^3 + c$$

> This is called the **general solution**, because it involves the constant c, i.e. a family of solutions.

The constant c can be found using the information that $y = 2$ when $x = 0$. Substituting gives

$$2 = 0 + c$$

$$\therefore \quad c = 2$$

The solution is $y = \sin x + x^3 + 2$.

> This is called the **particular solution**.

1.1 VARIABLES SEPARABLE

If a first-order differential equation can be written in the form

$$\frac{dy}{dx} = f(x,y) = h(x)\,g(y)$$

i.e. the function $f(x,y)$ can be expressed as the product of a function of x and a function of y, then the equation can be solved by the method known as 'variables separable'.

Example

Solve the differential equation $\dfrac{dy}{dx} = xy$.

Solution

Since $\dfrac{dy}{dx}$ is of the form $h(x)\,g(y)$, the variables can be separated.

Rearranging gives

$$\frac{1}{y}\frac{dy}{dx} = x$$

Integrating with respect to x gives

$$\int \frac{1}{y}dy = \int x\,dx$$

$$\therefore \qquad \ln y = \frac{x^2}{2} + c$$

In this case, the solution can be manipulated further to obtain y in terms of x. This gives

$$y = e^{\frac{x^2}{2} + c}$$

$$= e^{\frac{x^2}{2}}e^c$$

$$y = Ae^{\frac{x^2}{2}}, \text{ letting } A = e^c, \text{ since it is constant}$$

Example

Solve the differential equation $e^y\dfrac{dy}{dx} - 2x = 0$, given that $y = 0$ when $x = 1$.

Solution

Rearranging gives

$$\frac{dy}{dx} = \frac{2x}{e^y}$$

$$= 2x \times \frac{1}{e^y}, \text{ i.e. the form } h(x)\,g(y)$$

$\Rightarrow$ solve by 'separating variables'

Rearranging gives

$$e^y\frac{dy}{dx} = 2x$$

Integrating with respect to x:

$$\int e^y dy = \int 2x\,dx$$

$$e^y = x^2 + c$$

This is the general solution.

Using the fact that $y = 0$ when $x = 1$ enables the value of the constant to be found and gives

$$1 = (1)^2 + c$$

$$\therefore \quad c = 0$$

Therefore, we have

$$e^y = x^2$$

This can be manipulated further to obtain y in terms of x. This gives

$$y = \ln x^2$$

$$\therefore \quad y = 2\ln x$$

2 Applications

2.1 DISPLACEMENT, VELOCITY AND ACCELERATION

The velocity v of a body is defined as the rate of change of the displacement s of the body from some fixed orgin, with respect to time. This is given as

$$v = \frac{ds}{dt}$$

The acceleration a of a body is defined as the rate of change of the velocity of the body with respect to time. This is given as

$$a = \frac{dv}{dt} = \frac{d^2s}{dt^2}$$

It is useful to remember the following summary.

Differentiate with respect to time

s = displacement
v = velocity
a = acceleration

Integrate with respect to time

Example

A particle starts from a point O and moves in a straight line. Its velocity v, at time t, is given by $v = 5 + 6t - 3t^2$, where v is in metres per second and t is in seconds. Find

(i) its acceleration a at time t

(ii) the distance s from O at time t

(iii) the distance travelled in the second second

Solution

(i) The acceleration at time t is given by

$$a = \frac{dv}{dt} = 6 - 6t$$

(ii) The distance from O at time t is given by

$$s = \int v \, dt$$
$$= \int 5 + 6t - 3t^2 \, dt$$
$$= 5t + 3t^2 - t^3 + c$$

We know that the particle starts from O, i.e. $s = 0$ when $t = 0$. Substituting gives

$$c = 0$$

$$\therefore \quad s = 5t + 3t^2 - t^3$$

(iii) The distance travelled in the second second is given by

$$\int_1^2 5 + 6t - 3t^2 \, dt = \left[5t + 3t^2 - t^3 \right]_1^2$$

$$= 14 - 7$$

$$= 7$$

The distance travelled in the second second is 7 metres.

2.2 GROWTH AND DECAY

A common application of differential equations is to the laws of growth and decay.

- If the rate of growth of x is proportional to x, then $\frac{dx}{dt} = kx$, where k is a positive constant.

- If the rate of decay of x is proportional to x, then $\frac{dx}{dt} = -kx$, where k is a positive constant.

Example

For each of the following situations, write down the differential equation which it satisfies.

(i)   A population is increasing at a rate which is proportional to its size.

(ii) A dog runs such that its speed is always inversely proportional to its distance from the starting point.

Solution

(i)   Let N be the size of the population at time t. Then $\frac{dN}{dt} = kN$, where k is constant.

(ii) Let x be the distance from the starting point. We know that the dog's speed is given by $\frac{dx}{dt}$ and the differential equation is given by

$$\frac{dx}{dt} = k\frac{1}{x}, \text{ where } k \text{ is constant}$$

Note: when answering questions on differential equations, it is important to identify initial conditions (values for t and x, say). These are given to enable the unknown constants to be calculated. The following example illustrates exactly this.

Example

A mould grows at a rate proportional to its present size. Initially, there are 3 grams of this mould and three days later there are 5 grams. Predict how much mould will be present after five days.

Solution

Let N be the quantity of mould at time t. Then

$$\frac{dN}{dt} = kN, \text{ where } k \text{ is constant}$$

Using the method of 'variables separable' gives

$$\frac{1}{N}\frac{dN}{dt} = k$$

i.e $\int \frac{1}{N} dN = \int k \, dt$

$\ln N = kt + c$

$\therefore \qquad N = e^{kt+c}$

$\therefore \qquad N = Ae^{kt} \qquad (*)$

Using initial conditions ($t = 0$, $N = 3$) gives

$3 = Ae^0$

$\therefore \quad A = 3$

Returning to (*), we now have the model represented by

$N = 3e^{kt}$

> The second set of conditions is used to enable the remaining unknown constant k to be calculated.

When $t = 3$, $N = 5$, substituting gives

$5 = 3e^{3k}$

$\therefore \quad e^{3k} = \frac{5}{3}$

$3k = \ln\left(\frac{5}{3}\right)$

$\therefore \qquad k = \frac{1}{3}\ln\left(\frac{5}{3}\right)$

Now that the values of both constants are known, the equation used to model the situation is known and is given by

$N = 3e^{\frac{t}{3}\ln\left(\frac{5}{3}\right)}$

To find the amount of mould after five days, substitute $t = 5$, giving

$N = 3e^{5 \times \frac{5}{3}\ln\left(\frac{5}{3}\right)}$

$\therefore \quad N = 7.03 \text{ grams (2 dp)}$

2.3 NEWTON'S LAW OF COOLING

A common application of differential equations is to Newton's Law of Cooling. This states that the rate of change of the temperature of a body with respect to time is proportional to the temperature difference between the body and its surrounding medium.

This can be expressed in the form

$\frac{dT}{dt} = -kT$

where k is a constant and T is the amount by which the temperature of the body exceeds the temperature of its surrounding medium.

Example

A body at a temperature of 60°C is placed in an oven, the temperature of which is kept at 130°C. If after 10 minutes the temperature of the body is 80°C, find the time required for the body to reach a temperature of 100°C.

Solution

Using the differential equation $\dfrac{\mathrm{d}T}{\mathrm{d}t} = -kT$, and solving, gives

$$\frac{1}{T}\frac{\mathrm{d}T}{\mathrm{d}t} = -k$$

i.e. $\displaystyle\int \frac{1}{T}\mathrm{d}T = -\int k\,\mathrm{d}t$

$$\ln T = -kt + c$$

$$T = e^{-kt + c}$$

$\therefore \qquad T = Ae^{-kt}$

The unknown constants are A and k; conditions from the question need to be used to determine their values.

Initially $(t = 0)$, $T = 60° -130° = -70°$,

$\therefore \quad -70 = Ae^0$

$\therefore \qquad A = -70$

This gives the equation for the model as

$$T = -70e^{-kt}$$

When $t = 10$, $T = 80° -130° = -50°$,

$\therefore \qquad -50 = -70e^{-10k}$

$$e^{-10k} = \frac{5}{7}$$

$$-10k = \ln\left(\frac{5}{7}\right)$$

$\therefore \qquad k = -\dfrac{1}{10}\ln\left(\dfrac{5}{7}\right)$

The model is represented by the equation

$$T = -70e^{\frac{t}{10}\ln\left(\frac{5}{7}\right)}$$

When the body is at a temperature of 100°, we have $T = 100° -130° = -30°$. Substituting gives

$$-30° = -70e^{\frac{t}{10}\ln\left(\frac{5}{7}\right)}$$

$$e^{\frac{t}{10}\ln\left(\frac{5}{7}\right)} = \frac{3}{7}$$

$$\frac{t}{10}\ln\left(\frac{5}{7}\right) = \ln\left(\frac{3}{7}\right)$$

$$t = \frac{10\ln\left(\frac{3}{7}\right)}{\ln\left(\frac{5}{7}\right)}$$

$$t = 25.2 \text{ min (1 dp)}$$

Key points

- Differential equations of the form

  - $\dfrac{dy}{dx} = f(x)$ can be solved by integrating term by term

  - $\dfrac{dy}{dx} = h(x)\,g(y)$ can be solved using the 'variables separable' method

- The velocity v of a body is defined as the rate of change of the displacement s of the body from some fixed origin, with respect to time. This is given as

  $$v = \frac{ds}{dt}$$

- The acceleration a of a body is defined as the rate of change of the velocity of the body with respect to time. This is given as

  $$a = \frac{dv}{dt} = \frac{d^2s}{dt^2}$$

- If the rate of growth of x is proportional to x, then $\dfrac{dx}{dt} = kx$, where k is a positive constant.

- If the rate of decay of x is proportional to x, then $\dfrac{dx}{dt} = -kx$, where k is a positive constant.

- A particular application of differential equations is Newton's Law of Cooling.

- When using differential equations to model a situation, it is important to identify (i) initial conditions, usually corresponding to $t = 0$, and (ii) a second set of conditions, so that the values of the unknown constants can be determined.

1 Solving equations using numerical methods

1.1 LOCATING ROOTS

The roots of the equation $f(x) = 0$ can be located by considering the sign of $f(x)$, providing $f(x)$ is continuous.

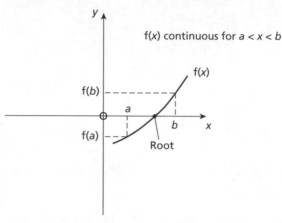

$\left.\begin{array}{l} f(a) < 0 \\ f(b) > 0 \end{array}\right\}$ the graph of $y = f(x)$ is continuous between a and b. Therefore, $f(x) = 0$ for some x value between a and b.

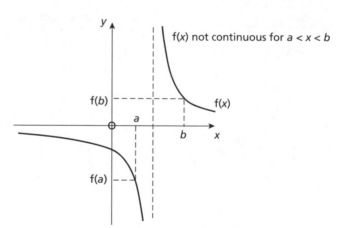

$\left.\begin{array}{l} f(a) < 0 \\ f(b) > 0 \end{array}\right\}$ the graph of $y = f(x)$ is *not* continous between a and b. Therefore, we cannot conclude that a root lies between a and b.

Example

Locate the interval in which the root of the equation $x^3 + 2x^2 - 2 = 0$ lies.

Solution

Although the equation $x^3 + 2x^2 - 2 = 0$ has no factors, it does have one real root. The following table of values corresponds to $f(x) = x^3 + 2x^2 - 2$:

x	-1	0	1	2
$f(x)$	-1	-2	1	14

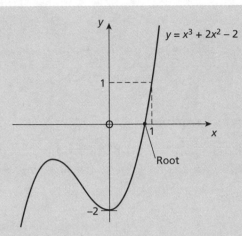

By inspection, the curve must cross the x-axis between 0 and 1 since $f(x)$ changes sign and we know that the graph of $f(x) = x^3 + 2x^2 - 2$ is continuous. Therefore, the equation $x^3 + 2x^2 - 2 = 0$ has a root in the interval $(0, 1)$.

1.2 BISECTION METHOD

This is a numerical method for finding the root of an equation to a required number of decimal places. It involves a continuous process of bisecting the interval in which the root lies.

Example

Locate the single root of the equation $x^3 + 2x^2 - 2 = 0$ and hence use the bisection method to find this root, correct to one decimal place.

Solution

Let $f(x) = x^3 + 2x^2 - 2$. We have already determined that the root lies between 0 and 1.

Bisecting the interval $(0, 1)$ gives 0.5 and $f(0.5) = -1.375 < 0$. Since $f(1) = 1 > 0$, we know that the root lies in the interval $(0.5, 1)$.

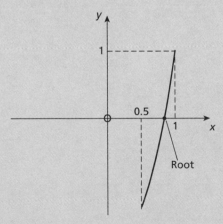

Continuing the process gives

$$f(0.75) = -0.4531 < 0 \Rightarrow \text{root lies in interval } (0.75, 1)$$

$$f(0.875) = 0.2012 > 0 \Rightarrow \text{root lies in interval } (0.75, 0.875)$$

$f(0.8125) = -0.1433 < 0 \Rightarrow$ root lies in interval $(0.8125, 0.875)$

$f(0.84375) = 0.0245 > 0 \Rightarrow$ root lies in interval $(0.8125, 0.84375)$

The required root is 0.8, to one decimal place.

1.3 ITERATIVE METHODS

An iterative formula can be obtained from the equation $f(x) = 0$ by rearranging into the form $x = F(x)$, which gives rise to the iterative formula

$$x_{r+1} = F(x_r)$$

If the graphs of $y = x$ and $y = F(x)$ are as shown below,

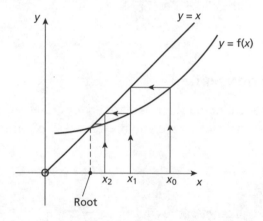

then we see that an initial value x_0 results in a converging sequence, $x_1, x_2, \ldots$

Note: a converging sequence is not always obtained.

Example

Show that the equation $x^3 + 2x^2 - 2 = 0$ can be rearranged into the form $x = \left(\frac{2}{x+2}\right)^{\frac{1}{2}}$. Hence, write down an iterative formula and, using a suitable initial value x_0, find the single root of the equation, correct to three decimal places.

Solution

Starting with $x^3 + 2x^2 - 2 = 0$ and factorising x^2 from the first two terms gives

$$x^2(x+2) - 2 = 0$$

$$\therefore \qquad x^2 = \frac{2}{x+2}$$

$$\therefore \qquad x = \left(\frac{2}{x+2}\right)^{\frac{1}{2}}$$

The resulting iterative formula is $x_{r+1} = \left(\frac{2}{x_r + 2}\right)^{\frac{1}{2}}$

Note: a graphical calculator is very useful for finding the resulting sequence and identifying convergence. Input the x_0 value into the calculator and then key in the iterative formula in the form $(2 \div (\text{ANS} + 2)) \wedge (0.5)$. Pressing EXE/ENTER repeatedly gives the sequence of terms.

Letting $x_0 = 1$ (since we know the root lies between 0 and 1) gives

$\quad x_1 = 0.816497$
$\quad x_2 = 0.842676$
$\quad x_3 = 0.838786$
$\quad x_4 = 0.839361$
$\quad x_5 = 0.839279$

The root is 0.839, to three decimal places.

Graphically,

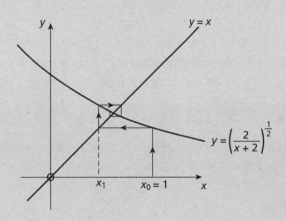

Note: not all rearrangements of the equation $f(x) = 0$ will give rise to iterative formulae that converge to the required root.

For instance, in the above example, consider the rearrangement $x = \frac{2}{x^2 + 2x}$, which gives the iterative formula $x_{r+1} = \frac{2}{x_r^2 + 2x_r}$.

Letting $x_0 = 1$ gives

$\quad x_1 = 0.6$
$\quad x_2 = 1.125$
$\quad x_3 = 0.568$
$\quad x_4 = 1.3685$
$\quad x_5 = 0.4338$
$\qquad 1.8941$
$\qquad \vdots$
$\quad\ 39.9480$
$\quad\ 0.0012$

It is clear that, in this case, the iterative formula is not converging but is 'jumping' about.

1.4 NEWTON–RAPHSON ITERATIVE FORMULA

- The Newton–Raphson iterative formula for solving the equation $f(x) = 0$ is given by

$$x_{r+1} = x_r - \frac{f(x_r)}{f'(x_r)}$$

Consider the graph of $y = f(x)$, as shown below:

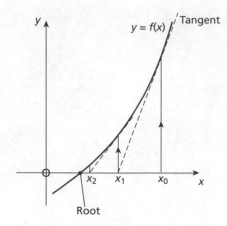

Root

If x_0 is the initial value, the intersection of the tangent line to $f(x)$ at $x = x_0$, with the x-axis gives x_1. This process is then repeated to obtain x_2, x_3 etc.

Example

Show that the equation $x - 2\sin x = 0$ has a root between 1 and 2. Use the Newton–Raphson method to determine this root, correct to three decimal places.

Solution

Remember to use radians.

Let $f(x) = x - 2\sin x$. Now, $f(1) < 0$ and $f(2) > 0$. Since we also know that $y = f(x)$ is continuous, there exists a root between 1 and 2.

For Newton–Raphson, we require the first derivative, $f'(x) = 1 - 2\cos x$. Therefore, the Newton–Raphson iterative formula is given by

$$x_{r+1} = x_r - \frac{(x_r - 2\sin x_r)}{(1 - 2\cos x_r)}$$

Letting $x_0 = 2$ gives

$x_1 = 1.9000$
$x_2 = 1.8955$
$x_3 = 1.8955$

The root is 1.896, to three decimal places.

Key points

● The roots of the equation $f(x) = 0$ can be located by considering the sign of $f(x)$ and looking for a change, providing $f(x)$ is continuous in the interval under consideration.

● **Bisection method:** this involves continual bisection of the interval in which the root lies.

● **Iterative methods:** these involve rearranging the equation $f(x) = 0$ into the form $x = F(x)$, which then gives rise to the iterative formula $x_{r+1} = F(x_r)$.

Note: usually there are many rearrangements of the equation $f(x) = 0$ to consider.

- **Newton-Raphson method:** this is a particular iterative formula that involves the first derivative,

$$x_{r+1} = x_r - \frac{f(x_r)}{f'(x_r)}$$

This usually provides a fast-converging sequence.

2 *Numerical integration*

2.1 TRAPEZIUM RULE

This gives the area A between the curve $y = f(x)$, the ordinates $x = a$ and $x = b$, and the x-axis as

$$A \approx \frac{h}{2}\{y_0 + 2(y_1 + y_2 + \ldots + y_{n-2}) + y_{n-1}\}$$

where $h = \dfrac{b - a}{n - 1}$ and $y_i = f(a + ih)$.

The approach is to split the required area into trapezia of equal width.

Note: if n is the number of ordinates, there are $(n - 1)$ trapezia or strips.

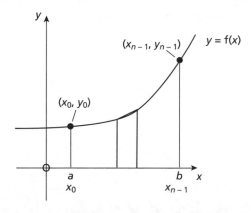

Example

Using the trapezium rule with three ordinates, find an estimate for the area under the curve $y = e^x$ between $x = 0$ and $x = 1$.

Solution

Now, $h = \dfrac{1 - 0}{3 - 1} = \dfrac{1}{2}$ (i.e. 3 ordinates but 2 trapezia)

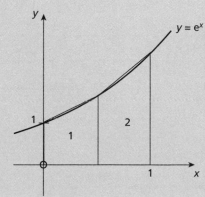

Therefore,

$$A \approx \frac{(\frac{1}{2})}{2} \{y_0 + 2y_1 + y_2\}$$

$$\approx \frac{1}{4}\{1 + 2(1.649) + 2.718\}$$

$$\approx 1.754$$

The area is approximately 1.75.

2.2 SIMPSON'S RULE

This gives the area A between the curve $y = f(x)$, the ordinates $x = a$ and $x = b$, and the x-axis as

$$A \approx \frac{1}{3}h\{y_0 + 4(y_1 + y_3 + \ldots + y_{n-2}) + 2(y_2 + y_4 + \ldots y_{n-3}) + y_{n-1}\}$$

where n is odd, $h = \frac{b-a}{n-1}$ and $y_i = f(a + ih)$.

This approach is to join the first three points (x_0, y_0), (x_1, y_1) and (x_2, y_2) by a parabola, the three points (x_2, y_2), (x_3, y_3) and (x_4, y_4) by a parabola and so on. It is now clear why the number of points needs to be odd.

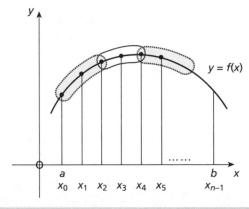

Example

Using Simpson's rule with seven ordinates, find an estimate for the area under the curve $y = \sqrt{1 + x^2}$ between $x = 1$ and 4.

Solution

Now $h = \frac{4-1}{7-1} = \frac{3}{6} = \frac{1}{2}$

Table of values:

x	1	1.5	2	2.5	3	3.5	4
y	1.41	1.80	2.24	2.69	3.16	3.64	4.12

By Simpson's rule,

$$A \approx \frac{(\frac{1}{2})}{3}\{1.41 + 4(1.80 + 2.69 + 3.64) + 2(2.24 + 3.16) + 4.12\}$$

$$A \approx 8.14$$

The area is approximately 8.14.

Key points

- **Trapezium rule:** this involves dividing the area under the curve into trapezia of equal width, constructing a table of values for the function appropriate to the number of ordinates and using the given formula.

- **Simpson's rule:** this involves joining consecutive sets of three points with a parabola (as shown on page 138), constructing a table of values for the function appropriate to the number of ordinates and using the given formula.

TOPIC 12 Vectors

1 Basics

- A **vector** is a quantity specified by a magnitude and a direction.

- A **scalar** is a quantity specified by magnitude only.

1.1 NOTATION

The vector shown below may be written as

$$\overrightarrow{OA} = \begin{pmatrix} 3 \\ 1 \end{pmatrix}, \text{ called a column vector}$$

$$\overrightarrow{OA} = 3\mathbf{i} + 1\mathbf{j}, \text{ using the unit vectors } \mathbf{i} = \begin{pmatrix} 1 \\ 0 \end{pmatrix} \text{ and } \mathbf{j} = \begin{pmatrix} 0 \\ 1 \end{pmatrix}$$

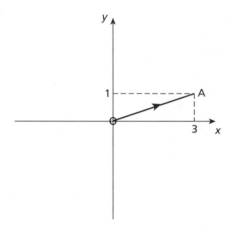

In three dimensions, similar notation can be used.

The vector $\mathbf{v} = \begin{pmatrix} 2 \\ 1 \\ -3 \end{pmatrix}$ can be written as $\mathbf{v} = 2\mathbf{i} + \mathbf{j} - 3\mathbf{k}$, using the unit vectors

$$\mathbf{i} = \begin{pmatrix} 1 \\ 0 \\ 0 \end{pmatrix}, \mathbf{j} = \begin{pmatrix} 0 \\ 1 \\ 0 \end{pmatrix} \text{ and } \mathbf{k} = \begin{pmatrix} 0 \\ 0 \\ 1 \end{pmatrix}.$$

- The magnitude of the vector $\mathbf{v} = \begin{pmatrix} a \\ b \\ c \end{pmatrix}$ is given by $|\mathbf{v}| = \sqrt{a^2 + b^2 + c^2}$.

- A **unit vector** is a vector of length 1.

Example

Find the magnitude of the vector $\mathbf{v} = \mathbf{i} - 2\mathbf{j} + 4\mathbf{k}$.

Solution

$$|\mathbf{v}| = \sqrt{1^2 + (-2)^2 + 4^2}$$
$$\therefore \quad |\mathbf{v}| = \sqrt{21}$$

Example

Find the unit vector in the direction of $\mathbf{v} = \mathbf{i} - 5\mathbf{j} + \mathbf{k}$.

Solution

$$|\mathbf{v}| = \sqrt{1^2 + (-5)^2 + 1^2}$$

$$\therefore \quad |\mathbf{v}| = \sqrt{27} = 3\sqrt{3}$$

Therefore, the unit vector in the direction of $\mathbf{v}$, denoted $\hat{\mathbf{v}}$, is given by

$$\hat{\mathbf{v}} = \frac{1}{3\sqrt{3}}\mathbf{v} = \frac{1}{3\sqrt{3}}\mathbf{i} - \frac{5}{3\sqrt{3}}\mathbf{j} + \frac{1}{3\sqrt{3}}\mathbf{k}$$

Example

Given that $\mathbf{v} = \begin{pmatrix} -1 \\ 6 \\ 2 \end{pmatrix}$, find $-2\mathbf{v}$ and state the geometrical relationship between the vectors $\mathbf{v}$ and $-2\mathbf{v}$.

Solution

$$-2\mathbf{v} = -2\begin{pmatrix} -1 \\ 6 \\ 2 \end{pmatrix} = \begin{pmatrix} 2 \\ -12 \\ -4 \end{pmatrix}$$

This vector is twice the length of vector $\mathbf{v}$, but has an opposite direction.

1.2 RESULTANT VECTORS

In the diagram shown below, the vector $\overrightarrow{AC}$ is the resultant of vectors $\overrightarrow{AB}$ and $\overrightarrow{BC}$.

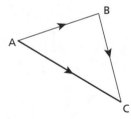

In other words, $\overrightarrow{AC} = \overrightarrow{AB} + \overrightarrow{BC}$.

Example

Given that $\mathbf{v} = \mathbf{i} + \mathbf{j} - 3\mathbf{k}$ and $\mathbf{w} = 5\mathbf{i} - \mathbf{j} + 2\mathbf{k}$, find

(i) $\mathbf{v} + \mathbf{w}$

(ii) $\mathbf{v} - \mathbf{w}$

Solution

(i) $\mathbf{v} + \mathbf{w} = (\mathbf{i} + \mathbf{j} - 3\mathbf{k}) + (5\mathbf{i} - \mathbf{j} + 2\mathbf{k})$
$$= 6\mathbf{i} - \mathbf{k}$$

(ii) $\mathbf{v} - \mathbf{w} = (\mathbf{i} + \mathbf{j} - 3\mathbf{k}) - (5\mathbf{i} - \mathbf{j} + 2\mathbf{k})$
$$= -4\mathbf{i} + 2\mathbf{j} - 5\mathbf{k}$$

TOPIC 12 Vectors

2 | Position vectors

The position vector of a point P with respect to a fixed origin O is the vector $\overrightarrow{OP}$.

It is usual to write $\overrightarrow{OP} = \mathbf{p}$.

Given two points A and B with position vectors $\mathbf{a}$ and $\mathbf{b}$ respectively, then

$$\overrightarrow{AB} = \overrightarrow{AO} + \overrightarrow{OB}$$

$$= -\mathbf{a} + \mathbf{b}$$

$$\therefore \quad \overrightarrow{AB} = \mathbf{b} - \mathbf{a}$$

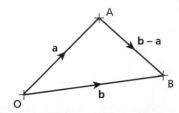

This is an extremely useful result and should be remembered.

Example

Given that A and B have coordinates $(-3, 2)$ and $(4, 1)$ respectively, find $\overrightarrow{AB}$ and hence the distance between the points A and B.

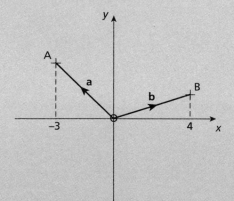

Solution

Now,

$$\overrightarrow{OA} = \mathbf{a} = \begin{pmatrix} -3 \\ 2 \end{pmatrix} \text{ and } \overrightarrow{OB} = \mathbf{b} = \begin{pmatrix} 4 \\ 1 \end{pmatrix}$$

Since $\overrightarrow{AB} = \mathbf{b} - \mathbf{a}$,

$$\overrightarrow{AB} = \begin{pmatrix} 4 \\ 1 \end{pmatrix} - \begin{pmatrix} -3 \\ 2 \end{pmatrix}$$

$$\therefore \quad \overrightarrow{AB} = \begin{pmatrix} 7 \\ -1 \end{pmatrix}$$

The distance AB is given by the magnitude of the vector $\overrightarrow{AB}$.

Now,

$$|\overrightarrow{AB}| = \sqrt{7^2 + (-1)^2} = \sqrt{50}$$

$$\therefore \quad |\overrightarrow{AB}| = 5\sqrt{2}$$

The distance between A and B is $5\sqrt{2}$.

Example

OABC is a rectangle with $\overrightarrow{OA} = \mathbf{a}$ and $\overrightarrow{OB} = \mathbf{b}$. P is the point on AB such that AP : PB is 2 : 1. Find

(i) $\overrightarrow{OP}$

(ii) $\overrightarrow{PC}$

in terms of the vectors $\mathbf{a}$ and $\mathbf{b}$.

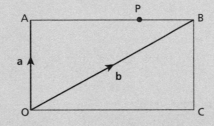

Solution

(i) $\quad \overrightarrow{OP} = \overrightarrow{OA} + \overrightarrow{AP}$

$$= \overrightarrow{OA} + \frac{2}{3}\overrightarrow{AB}$$

$$= \mathbf{a} + \frac{2}{3}(\mathbf{b} - \mathbf{a})$$

$$= \mathbf{a} + \frac{2}{3}\mathbf{b} - \frac{2}{3}\mathbf{a}$$

$$\therefore \quad \overrightarrow{OP} = \frac{1}{3}\mathbf{a} + \frac{2}{3}\mathbf{b}$$

$$\therefore \quad \overrightarrow{OP} = \frac{1}{3}(\mathbf{a} + 2\mathbf{b})$$

(ii) $\quad \overrightarrow{PC} = \overrightarrow{PO} + \overrightarrow{OC}$

$$= -\frac{1}{3}(\mathbf{a} + 2\mathbf{b}) + \overrightarrow{AB}, \text{ since } \overrightarrow{OC} \text{ is the same length and has the same}$$
$$\text{direction as } \overrightarrow{AB}$$

$$= -\frac{1}{3}(\mathbf{a} + 2\mathbf{b}) + (\mathbf{b} - \mathbf{a})$$

$$= \frac{1}{3}\mathbf{b} - \frac{4}{3}\mathbf{a}$$

$$\therefore \quad \overrightarrow{PC} = \frac{1}{3}(\mathbf{b} - 4\mathbf{a})$$

3 | _Scalar product_

- The scalar product **a.b** of two vectors **a** and **b** is defined by

$$\mathbf{a.b} = |\mathbf{a}|\,|\mathbf{b}|\cos\theta$$

where θ is the angle between the vectors.

- When the two vectors **a** and **b** are perpendicular, **a.b** = 0.

Example

Find the scalar product of the two vectors $\mathbf{a} = \mathbf{i} - 3\mathbf{j} + \mathbf{k}$ and $\mathbf{b} = 2\mathbf{i} + \mathbf{j} - 4\mathbf{k}$.

Solution

$$\mathbf{a.b} = (1 \times 2) + (-3 \times 1) + (1 \times -4) = -5$$

The scalar product is -5.

Example

Find the angle between the vectors $\mathbf{a} = 2\mathbf{i} + \mathbf{j} - 2\mathbf{k}$ and $\mathbf{b} = \mathbf{i} - \mathbf{j} + \mathbf{k}$.

Solution

Using $\mathbf{a.b} = |\mathbf{a}|\,|\mathbf{b}|\cos\theta$, gives

$$(2 \times 1) + (1 \times (-1)) + (-2 \times 1) = \sqrt{2^2 + 1^2 + (-2)^2}\,\sqrt{1^2 + (-1)^2 + 1^2}\cos\theta$$

$$-1 = 3\sqrt{3}\cos\theta$$

$$\therefore \qquad \cos\theta = -\frac{1}{3\sqrt{3}}$$

$$\therefore \qquad \theta = 101.1°$$

The angle between the two vectors is $101.1°$.

Key points

- The magnitude (length) of the vector $\mathbf{v} = \begin{pmatrix} a \\ b \\ c \end{pmatrix}$ is given by $|\mathbf{v}| = \sqrt{a^2 + b^2 + c^2}$.

- A unit vector is a vector of length 1.

- The resultant of vectors **a** and **b** is **a** + **b**.

- If A and B are two points with position vectors **a** and **b**, then $\overrightarrow{AB} = \mathbf{b} - \mathbf{a}$.

- The scalar product of two vectors **a** and **b** is defined as $\mathbf{a.b} = |\mathbf{a}|\,|\mathbf{b}|\cos\theta$, where θ is the angle between the vectors.

- When two vectors **a** and **b** are perpendicular, **a.b** = 0.

4 Lines

4.1 Vector equation of a line

If **a** and **b** are the position vectors of two points A and B with respect to an origin O, the vector equation of the line AB is given by

$$\mathbf{r} = \mathbf{a} + t\,(\mathbf{b} - \mathbf{a})$$

where t is a scalar.

Note: when $t = 0$, $\mathbf{r} = \mathbf{a}$ and when $t = 1$, $\mathbf{r} = \mathbf{b}$.

Example

Find the vector equation of the line passing through the points A $(2, 5)$ and B $(-3, 7)$.

Solution

We have $\mathbf{a} = \begin{pmatrix} 2 \\ 5 \end{pmatrix}$ and $\mathbf{b} = \begin{pmatrix} -3 \\ 7 \end{pmatrix}$. The vector equation of the line is given by

$$\mathbf{r} = \mathbf{a} + t\,(\mathbf{b} - \mathbf{a})$$
$$= \begin{pmatrix} 2 \\ 5 \end{pmatrix} + t\left\{ \begin{pmatrix} -3 \\ 7 \end{pmatrix} - \begin{pmatrix} 2 \\ 5 \end{pmatrix} \right\}$$
$$\therefore \quad \mathbf{r} = \begin{pmatrix} 2 \\ 5 \end{pmatrix} + t \begin{pmatrix} -5 \\ 2 \end{pmatrix}$$

4.2 Intersection of two lines

- In two dimensions, two straight lines either:
  - intersect at a point, or
  - are parallel, i.e. have the same direction

- In three dimensions, two straight lines:
  - intersect at a point, or
  - are parallel, or
  - are skew, i.e. non-parallel lines that do not meet

Example

Decide whether the following pairs of lines intersect, are parallel or are skew.

(i) $\mathbf{r}_1 = \begin{pmatrix} 1 \\ 5 \end{pmatrix} + t \begin{pmatrix} -2 \\ 5 \end{pmatrix}$; $\mathbf{r}_2 = \begin{pmatrix} -1 \\ 7 \end{pmatrix} + s \begin{pmatrix} 3 \\ -6 \end{pmatrix}$

(ii) $\mathbf{r}_1 = (3\mathbf{i} + 5\mathbf{j} + 7\mathbf{k}) + t\,(2\mathbf{i} + 3\mathbf{j} + 5\mathbf{k})$; $\mathbf{r}_2 = (\mathbf{i} + 2\mathbf{j} + 3\mathbf{k}) + s\,(\mathbf{i} + 2\mathbf{j} + \mathbf{k})$

Solution

(i) At intersection,

$$\mathbf{r}_1 = \mathbf{r}_2$$

i.e. $\begin{pmatrix} 1 \\ 5 \end{pmatrix} + t \begin{pmatrix} -2 \\ 5 \end{pmatrix} = \begin{pmatrix} -1 \\ 7 \end{pmatrix} + s \begin{pmatrix} 3 \\ -6 \end{pmatrix}$

$$\begin{pmatrix} 1 - 2t \\ 5 + 5t \end{pmatrix} = \begin{pmatrix} -1 + 3s \\ 7 - 6s \end{pmatrix}$$

$\therefore \quad 1 - 2t = -1 + 3s$ and $5 + 5t = 7 - 6s$

$\therefore \quad 2 - 2t = 3s$ and $6s = 2 - 5t$

Solving simultaneously gives $s = 2$ and $t = -2$. The two lines **intersect**.

> Note: the position vector of the point of intersection can be found by substituting for s or t:
>
> $\mathbf{r} = \begin{pmatrix} 1 \\ 5 \end{pmatrix} + (-2)\begin{pmatrix} -2 \\ 5 \end{pmatrix}$, substituting the t value into $\mathbf{r}_1$
>
> $\therefore \mathbf{r} = \begin{pmatrix} 1 \\ 5 \end{pmatrix} + \begin{pmatrix} 4 \\ -10 \end{pmatrix}$
>
> $\therefore \mathbf{r} = \begin{pmatrix} 5 \\ -5 \end{pmatrix}$

(ii) At intersection,

$$\mathbf{r}_1 = \mathbf{r}_2$$

i.e. $\quad \begin{pmatrix} 3 \\ 5 \\ 7 \end{pmatrix} + t\begin{pmatrix} 2 \\ 3 \\ 5 \end{pmatrix} = \begin{pmatrix} 1 \\ 2 \\ 3 \end{pmatrix} + s\begin{pmatrix} 1 \\ 2 \\ 1 \end{pmatrix}$

$$\begin{pmatrix} 3 + 2t \\ 5 + 3t \\ 7 + 5t \end{pmatrix} = \begin{pmatrix} 1 + s \\ 2 + 2s \\ 3 + s \end{pmatrix}$$

$\therefore \quad 3 + 2t = 1 + s, \; 5 + 3t = 2 + 2s$ and $7 + 5t = 3 + s$

Solving these simultaneously shows that although $(s = 0, t = -1)$ satisfy the first two equations, the third is not satisfied by these values. There is no single set of values for s and t that will satisfy all three equations.

If the lines do not intersect, there are only two possibilities remaining — they are either parallel or skew.

These lines are not parallel, since the direction vectors, i.e. $\begin{pmatrix} 2 \\ 3 \\ 5 \end{pmatrix}$ and $\begin{pmatrix} 1 \\ 2 \\ 1 \end{pmatrix}$, are not multiples of each other.

Therefore, the two lines are **skew**.

5 Planes

5.1 VECTOR EQUATION OF A PLANE

Form 1

The vector equation of a plane is given by

$$\mathbf{r} = \mathbf{a} + \lambda\mathbf{b} + \mu\mathbf{c}$$

where $\mathbf{a}$ is the position vector of a point on the plane, and $\mathbf{b}$ and $\mathbf{c}$ are two non-parallel vectors in the plane.

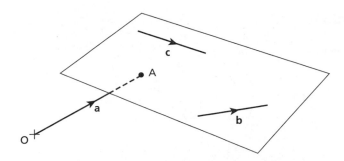

Form 2

The vector equation of a plane is given by

$$\mathbf{r} \cdot \mathbf{n} = \mathbf{a} \cdot \mathbf{n} = d$$

where $\mathbf{n}$ is a vector perpendicular to the plane, $\mathbf{a}$ is the position vector of a point on the plane and d is a constant.

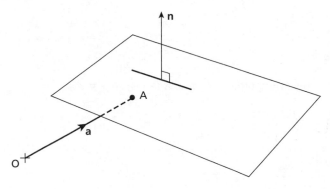

Form 3

The Cartesian form of the equation of a plane is

$$ax + by + cz = d$$

where a, b, c, and d are constants.

Example

Find the vector equation of the plane through the point $(1, 2, 1)$ which is

perpendicular to the vector $\mathbf{n} = \begin{pmatrix} 2 \\ 1 \\ -1 \end{pmatrix}$.

Solution

We have $\mathbf{a} = \begin{pmatrix} 1 \\ 2 \\ 1 \end{pmatrix}$ and $\mathbf{n} = \begin{pmatrix} 2 \\ 1 \\ -1 \end{pmatrix}$. Using form 2, the vector equation of the plane is given by

$$\mathbf{r} \cdot \mathbf{n} = \mathbf{a} \cdot \mathbf{n} = d$$

$$\therefore \quad \mathbf{r} \cdot \begin{pmatrix} 2 \\ 1 \\ -1 \end{pmatrix} = \begin{pmatrix} 1 \\ 2 \\ 1 \end{pmatrix} \cdot \begin{pmatrix} 2 \\ 1 \\ -1 \end{pmatrix}$$

$$\therefore \quad \mathbf{r} \cdot \begin{pmatrix} 2 \\ 1 \\ -1 \end{pmatrix} = 3$$

Example

Find the vector equation of the plane through the points A $(1, 2, 1)$, B $(1, 3, -2)$ and C $(4, -1, 2)$.

Solution

The vectors in the plane are

$$\overrightarrow{AB} = \mathbf{b} - \mathbf{a} = \begin{pmatrix} 1 \\ 3 \\ -2 \end{pmatrix} - \begin{pmatrix} 1 \\ 2 \\ 1 \end{pmatrix} = \begin{pmatrix} 0 \\ 1 \\ -3 \end{pmatrix}$$

$$\overrightarrow{BC} = \mathbf{c} - \mathbf{b} = \begin{pmatrix} 4 \\ -1 \\ 2 \end{pmatrix} - \begin{pmatrix} 1 \\ 3 \\ -2 \end{pmatrix} = \begin{pmatrix} 3 \\ -4 \\ 4 \end{pmatrix}$$

Now, choosing A $(1, 2, 1)$ as a point on the plane and using form 1, the vector equation is given by

$$\mathbf{r} = \begin{pmatrix} 1 \\ 2 \\ 1 \end{pmatrix} + \lambda \begin{pmatrix} 0 \\ 1 \\ -3 \end{pmatrix} + \mu \begin{pmatrix} 3 \\ -4 \\ 4 \end{pmatrix}$$

Example

Find the Cartesian equation of the plane $\mathbf{r} \cdot \begin{pmatrix} 2 \\ 4 \\ -1 \end{pmatrix} = 3$.

Solution

Let $\mathbf{r} = \begin{pmatrix} x \\ y \\ z \end{pmatrix}$ then

$$\begin{pmatrix} x \\ y \\ z \end{pmatrix} \cdot \begin{pmatrix} 2 \\ 4 \\ -1 \end{pmatrix} = 3$$

$$\therefore \quad 2x + 4y - z = 3$$

The Cartesian equation of the plane is $2x + 4y - z = 3$.

5.2 ANGLE BETWEEN TWO PLANES

The angle between two planes is the same as the angle between the vectors perpendicular to the planes.

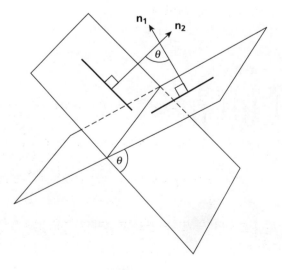

Example

Find the angle between the planes $\mathbf{r}_1 \cdot \begin{pmatrix} 2 \\ 5 \\ -1 \end{pmatrix} = 2$ and $\mathbf{r}_2 \cdot \begin{pmatrix} 3 \\ 1 \\ 6 \end{pmatrix} = 6$.

Solution

We need the angle between the vectors $\begin{pmatrix} 2 \\ 5 \\ -1 \end{pmatrix}$ and $\begin{pmatrix} 3 \\ 1 \\ 6 \end{pmatrix}$. Using the scalar product gives

$$\begin{pmatrix} 2 \\ 5 \\ -1 \end{pmatrix} \cdot \begin{pmatrix} 3 \\ 1 \\ 6 \end{pmatrix} = \sqrt{2^2 + 5^2 + (-1)^2}\,\sqrt{3^2 + 1^2 + 6^2}\,\cos\theta$$

$$\therefore \qquad 5 = \sqrt{30}\,\sqrt{46}\,\cos\theta$$

$$\therefore \qquad \theta = 82.3°$$

The angle between the two planes is $82.3°$.

5.3 ANGLE BETWEEN A LINE AND A PLANE

The angle between a line and a plane is given by $90° - \theta$, where θ is the angle between the line and the vector perpendicular to the plane.

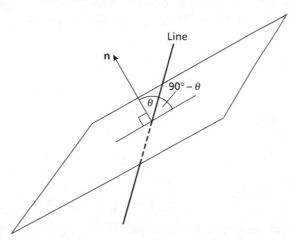

Example

Find the angle between the line $\mathbf{r} = (\mathbf{i} - \mathbf{j} + 3\mathbf{k}) + t(2\mathbf{i} - \mathbf{k})$ and the plane $2x + y - 3z = 5$.

Solution

The line $\mathbf{r} = \begin{pmatrix} 1 \\ -1 \\ 3 \end{pmatrix} + t\begin{pmatrix} 2 \\ 0 \\ -1 \end{pmatrix}$ has direction the same as the vector $\begin{pmatrix} 2 \\ 0 \\ -1 \end{pmatrix}$.

The plane $2x + y - 3z = 5$ can be written in the form $\mathbf{r} \cdot \begin{pmatrix} 2 \\ 1 \\ -3 \end{pmatrix} = 5$.

We need the angle between the vectors $\begin{pmatrix} 2 \\ 0 \\ -1 \end{pmatrix}$ and $\begin{pmatrix} 2 \\ 1 \\ -3 \end{pmatrix}$. Using the scalar product gives

$$\begin{pmatrix} 2 \\ 0 \\ -1 \end{pmatrix} \cdot \begin{pmatrix} 2 \\ 1 \\ -3 \end{pmatrix} = \sqrt{2^2 + (-1)^2}\,\sqrt{2^2 + 1^2 + (-3)^2}\,\cos\theta$$

$$\therefore \qquad\qquad 7 = \sqrt{5}\,\sqrt{14}\,\cos\theta$$

$$\therefore \qquad\qquad \theta = 33.2°$$

Therefore, the angle between the given line and plane is $90° - 33.2° = 56.8°$.

Key points

- $\mathbf{r} = \mathbf{a} + t\,(\mathbf{b} - \mathbf{a})$ is the vector equation of a line which passes through two points A,B with position vectors $\mathbf{a}$ and $\mathbf{b}$ respectively.

- To determine whether two lines intersect, are parallel or are skew (in the case of three dimensions), solve $\mathbf{r}_1 = \mathbf{r}_2$.

- Three forms of the equation of a plane are:
  (i) $\mathbf{r} = a + \lambda b + \mu c$
  (ii) $\mathbf{r} \cdot \mathbf{n} = \mathbf{a} \cdot \mathbf{n} = d$
  (iii) $ax + by + cz = d$

- The angle between two planes is the same as the angle between the vectors perpendicular to the planes.

- The angle between a line and a plane is given by $90° - \theta$, where θ is the angle between the line and the vector perpendicular to the plane.